THE KNOWING

AWAKE IN THE DARK: A SPIRITUAL MEMOIR

NITA LAPINSKI

ACKNOWLEDGMENTS

For my children whose inner strength and self-awareness constantly amaze me. May this book help you to heal and grow. Thank you for your love and support.

For my husband, I love you so.

Special thanks to Carly Kite for your encouragement, support and guidance.

My deepest gratitude to John DeDakis who's editing inspired me to be a better writer. And to Taylor Scott for making things flow seamlessly.

And lastly, to the group of listeners who let me read paragraph after paragraph until I got it right. Thank you.

PRAISE FOR NITA LAPINSKI

"A courageous story of one woman's journey from hell to healing and the intuitive gifts she discovers along the way."

- Sunny Dawn Johnston, author of *Invoking the Archangels - A Nine-Step Process to Healing Your Body, Mind, and Soul*

"Nita Lapinski has written a powerful story. The Knowing is raw and gripping. It is a book for our great era because it asks us all to see through the veil of pain and struggle to reveal our true gifts. Ms. Lapinski weaves a tale so compelling and honest that readers will identify with the struggle immediately. Ultimately, it is a story of liberation, healing and joy. What an honor to welcome Nita Lapinski into the fresh tribe of world-changing authors now coming forward to share their work."

- Jacob Nordby, speaker and author of *The Divine Arsonist: A Tale of Awakening*

PREFACE

Note to my readers

This is a true story about a painful period in my life. A period that feels as though it happened to someone else, a lifetime ago. I have not altered the unfolding of any events. Don't let my tumultuous past or unique gifts distract you from the real meaning of my account—it's not about tragedy or triumphs- it's about something much more.

I am a person whose life is easily judged, and if you feel anger or resentment, screaming your displeasure onto the pages, I'll understand. You may discover a piece of your own life or of someone you love, and through it, you may decide to forgive.

All names, except mine, have been changed to protect their privacy. I take creative liberty when speaking in the voice of the victims other than myself and rely on my intuition for insight into what may have occurred during their attacks. When describing the assaults, I have used court documents and police reports as reference.

The voice of the perpetrator in this narrative is based on actual knowledge and experience. The crimes he committed and their circumstances remain unchanged and authentic.

PROLOGUE

Falling mist floated sideways on the breeze, its evidence visible in the soft yellow glow of the street lamp. An invader with malicious intent hid behind a truck, a towing boom fixed to the bed. His face was covered with a mask. Only his eyes shone through the carefully cut out holes embroidered with bright orange thread on a black knit ski mask. Parked at the end of a building, the man had a clear view of an alley where the rear doors of its businesses sat firmly closed to the dreary weather and darkening night.

Rain pooled in the asphalt's potholes, its fresh scent mingling with the pungent smell of wet rubber rising up from the tires. Craning his neck, the man peered around the truck.

His neck muscles pulled and I felt the ache in his arm and knee and the dryness that filled his mouth. He was antsy and impatient hiding in the dark. His heart pumped steadily with excitement. I heard his rambling thoughts as if they were my own.

That bitch better hurry up, he thought. I don't have all night.

His jaw muscle popped as he ground his teeth and rubbed his elbow to relieve the throbbing there. The alley remained dark and deserted with only a hollow echo of water dripping from the roof to the blacktop below.

Without warning, the sharp scraping of metal against the pavement rang out. I saw the dark tip of a woman's high-heeled shoe and felt her toe wedged between the shop's heavy door and its frame. Her breath floated in the mist as she struggled to squeeze through.

In that moment, beneath the mask, the man smiled, his teeth exposed as they rubbed against the stretchy fabric that tightened across his lips.

Suddenly I became aware of my surroundings. I sat squeezed onto the corner of the couch, absently fingering the frayed, dirty pages of a worn paperback. I was having a vision. A sick feeling of dread lodged itself in my swollen, pregnant belly. The man in the mask felt familiar. *Do I know him somehow*? I thought as my mind searched for a clue. Fear restricted my ability to breathe. *This is not real,* my mind repeated again and again, *I'm imagining things again. I always do.*

Just seventeen-years-old and five months pregnant, years would pass before I sat sweating and afraid interviewed in front of a female sheriff's deputy. She was short with dark hair and eyes. Her gaze demanded my attention. She leaned forward and pushed a tape recorder toward me.

"Please state your full name."

"Nita McKenna," I'd said, feeling stupid and uncomfortable.

The officer sought to establish my connection with a serial rapist who, it would turn out, I knew very well. We would talk about his crimes, but I would not reveal my vision, afraid to admit I *knew*.

Pictures, as I called them or visions, had been happening randomly since early childhood. The vision of the man in the mask was not my first, and the realization of what I'd seen would haunt me for years. I was young and disbelieving when the vision came. I'd rejected it. I was afraid. I couldn't cope with the truth of what it meant. I would eventually realize who I saw, but it would take two decades before I fully understood the sickening significance.

THE BOY

Before he became the man in the mask- a man with anger that burned in his ears- he was a sweet and sensitive boy with a father as mean as a rabid badger.

The boy was seven the day his father came home drunk, angry that his lunch wasn't waiting for him on the table. He was a massive man with long arms, meaty fingers and perpetual redness in his cheeks. His meanness was as dense as swamp water, and his breath reeked with bitterness and rage. He glared hatefully at the boy and thumped him hard on the back of his head, yelling,

"Now you get outside, boy and clean up them weeds! I don't want to see no weeds in my yard. Get a move on."

The boy's stomach squirmed as he hurried outside. In the glaring mid-day sun, he did his best, but nothing could satisfy his father.

Stumbling onto the covered patio, the giant man threw open a chest filled with the treasures of boys. He dug like an animal, throwing baseballs and mitts, mallets for croquet, and wooden bats pitted and dark. He shoveled wildly until the contents of the chest lay scattered and meaningless across the cement porch.

Picking up the empty chest he slammed it down hard beyond the shade of the overhang, leaving it empty in the sun.

"Is that the best you can do, boy?" he said as he spat tobacco juice in the dirt.

In two strides he reached the boy and snatched him by the back of his shirt, hoisting him easily off the ground. The red-and- white striped fabric pulled tight against the boy's narrow chest. The father dropped the terrified child into the footlocker and slammed it closed. His breath came in hard gasps as he spotted a curved wire and twisted it through the shiny hardware clasp ensuring the chest couldn't be opened from the inside.

"That'll do it," he growled as he wiped the spit from the corner of his mouth.

The boy whimpered and cried, "I'll do it better, Daddy, I swear. Please, let me out. Daddy, please, I'm scared of the dark," he whispered.

By the time the boy's mother, Bernadette, rescued her youngest son from the dark and sweltering chest, he was limp and nearly unconscious. She carried him into the house and cradled him in her lap, wiping his head with a cool cloth and feeding him water. She whispered in the boy's ear,

"You got to stay away from him now, you hear me? Oh my lord," she murmured, "please God, don't let him kill my boy."

But it wouldn't be the last time the boy was locked in the chest, and with each cruel encounter the hateful intent of his father would begin to creep into the boy's own heart and begin to grow.

1

I was skeptical. I knew I shouldn't go. My stomach churned with warning but in the next moment I heard myself say, "Okay, Aaron, but just for a talk and that's all. Mom!" I called, "I'm going out with Aaron, but I'll be right back. Raine's asleep for the night." Not waiting for her reply, I quickly left the house with Aaron.

At seventeen, I'd taken my three-month-old baby, Raine, and moved back in with my mother. It'd been two years since I'd lived at home and I was surprised at the comfort I felt at being back. All I ever wanted—or so I thought—was to live with Aaron, Raine's father. For the past year and half my dream had come true. But I quickly discovered in him a volatile temper and vulgar tongue. I hadn't seen or spoken to Aaron since the morning I walked out on him, weeks before.

We drove on unlit back roads with the windows down. my long hair lashed at my face with sharp whips as Aaron made his case.

"I know I've been a jerk and I'm sorry. I'll change, just come home."

My emotions swirled. All I ever wanted was for Aaron to love me, to want me. He was finally asking, but his violent outbursts were terrifying and I was afraid for my son- I didn't want him to be like his father.

I bit down chewing on the soft pallet of my cheek. "No Aaron, we can't. I just can't." I said.

Suddenly his energy shifted. His anger erupted. His very person disappeared, replaced by billowing rage. a hateful smirk crept over his face as he gripped the steering wheel, increasing his speed.

He pushed down hard on the accelerator, babbling incoherently as the car flew down the road. The black silhouettes of trees and hills became a blur.

"Dammit, Nita! Are you already screwing someone?! I knew it! I knew you were!" he screamed, pounding the steering wheel.

"No Aaron! Jesus Christ, you're unbelievable!" My fingers tingled, my heart beat wildly, and my mouth lost its spit.

"I mean it!" He bellowed, "If I can't have you, then no one will! I will kill us both!"

I gripped the door handle. *Oh my god, what is he doing?* I was afraid of Aaron but I knew I was not alone in that car. I felt a presence with me. I called it "the light-body" and I'd been aware of it since puberty. The energy seemed to appear during stressful or dangerous situations but I hadn't put those pieces together yet. The light-body, along with the voice in my mind and the feeling in my gut (my *knowing*) told me, *you'll be safe.*

Instead of terror I felt calm wash over me as our speed increased. My seatbelt was secured, although it was uncommon to wear them at that time.

Aaron jerked the wheel to the right and we careened off the road. While in a free-fall, my world went silent. We hit a deep embankment where the groan of metal and shattered glass was a faraway sound.

The car dipped sharply to the left, crushing the driver's side door closed. Its nose was fixed securely in the ditch, causing the hood to wrinkle like a crushed coke can. Aaron was cursing and throwing his weight helplessly against a door that wouldn't budge. I released my belt and crawled, unhurt, through the passenger side window. I fled giving no thought to Aaron still struggling in the car.

Why do I always give into him? I wondered. What power does he have over me?

The night was an inky black. The back road was without street-lights, houses or traffic. I ran. The area was vaguely familiar. We were on the outskirts of an adjacent town, a predominantly black and poor area.

I half ran and half walked, barefoot, for about a mile when the bright sign of a twenty–four-hour store glowed in the distance. The unmistakable slang of black youths - whom I'd been conditioned to believe were unpredictable and dangerous - could be heard in the chill of the still night air. In front of the store in the glare of neon lights were groups of young black men drinking and loitering and selling drugs to late night patrons in search of an extended high on a Friday night. Wary and shaken, I had no coat or shoes to guard against the increasing chill.

No taunts or catcalls rang out, as I'd feared. Rather an unspoken understanding passed silently between us. I was a young girl in trouble and in need of help. A pay phone hung on the outside wall and beside it stood a man in a ragged knit cap. His eyes were blood-shot with droopy lids and the shine of an addict. His wordless appraisal rolled over me like a second skin as he dug in his pocket and pulled out a coin, extending his hand. The stark contrast of black skin against the white of his teeth struck me. I felt like I knew this complete stranger. I felt safe and I was grateful for the unexpected help.

It was past midnight when I awakened my sister Maggie with my desperate call. She came without comment or complaint. My mother was waiting up for us when we arrived home and said,

"When are you going to learn that he is dangerous? You're lucky he didn't kill you. Stay away from him, Nita, or he will."

She stood rigid, her arms crossed tightly over her breast. I gazed at her and saw disapproval spin like shiny lures around her body. The ability to see the energy that surrounded every living thing had been with me my entire life. Her hatred of him was visceral.

Aaron's attempt to hurt me was not his first or his last, and the severity of his efforts would grow. But don't let me confuse you by jumping ahead. Let me start slowly. Let's begin years before at church, the day God burst through the room.

2

I fixed my gaze on the church ceiling, as random lights exploded across the room. Seven years old, I kicked my legs back and forth like scissors, enjoying the whoosh of air they created as they swung. Dry coughs echoed in the church while parishioners dressed in stiff Sunday fabrics wiggled on hard, wooden pews. I waited for the shooting star to fly across the sanctuary ceiling a second time. I was sure it was God.

Suddenly the light zigzagged like lightning above our heads, silent in its flight. I was mesmerized. I turned to see who else had noticed the dazzling display, but all eyes were on the bishop, his voice booming. At that age it never occurred to me that others didn't see what I saw.

For as long as I can remember, I have always been able to see and hear things that most people do not. Over time, I have learned to uncover and understand my abilities, like the feeling that settles into your gut as the hair rises on your body exposing an unknown truth that invades you like a final breath. The ability to see the light I saw as a child is a form of clairvoyance called the Clairs. The Clairs are spiritual senses that come in five forms. Their gifts create an ability to witness past, present, and future events through visions that deliver unknowable information carried by a voice or sound. The Clairs bring the smell of a loved one who's passed, and the *knowing* of a stranger's illness, or deepest secret of a stranger.

All people are born with at least one of the Clairs, but for some of us, the abilities are naturally stronger. It's no different than a person who is born a natural athlete, artist, dancer or musician, deeply talented but untrained. They need to practice their skill and learn technique, but most importantly they need to believe in themselves.

The Clairs molded my life in a unique way that took time to understand and accept. My abilities created an odd mix of *knowing* and confusion. Having the Clairs didn't change the swollen purple bruises from a violent beating, or the pain of adolescence, or the shame and isolation of rape. My gifts didn't stop the progression of self-hate, or curb my promiscuous behavior, or prevent me from devouring dangerous drugs in an effort to blot out my miserable life. And the powerful Clairs did not keep me from getting pregnant at sixteen.

What they did was offer an intuition that revealed to me a person's inner feelings. Frequently in childhood, even though I *knew* how a person felt, it was beyond my emotional maturity level to understand why they felt that way. Likewise, I might have a vision or *picture* that I wasn't able to fully grasp, but the experience would reside in me for years. From a young age, my view of the world was unconventional. I *knew* there was a deeper meaning to what I experienced, but it would take decades for me to understand the significance.

I did my best to deny the Clairs when I was an adolescent. I quickly learned that having them made me different, and so I ignored the visions and the voices. In the end, it was the *knowing* that told me the events of my life were purposeful. *You can create your life,* the voice whispered, *you really can.* I recall hearing these types of messages most frequently in church but eventually the voice spilled over into every area of my life.

Raised as a Mormon, I often felt like a fraud. I broke God's rules on a regular basis. I lied to garner attention, stole my sister's things, and was envious of what others had. And that was just the beginning.

One Sunday in a stuffy, over heated room in the basement of our church, Mrs. Keller, our teacher, said, "God sits on His throne in heaven where He can see everything. He has a book with your name in it and writes down everything you do. You can't fool God."

With pursed lips she clutched the Book of Mormon and looked at each one of us as we squirmed uncomfortably in our chairs.

It was then that I heard a voice say, Not true. Don't be afraid, God doesn't sit on a throne or have a book with your name in it. Don't worry. God loves you no matter what.

At other times I might hear a response to something that was said directly to me.

"If you say swear words," warned a man in our church congregation, "God will make your teeth fall out so everyone will see that you swear. Swearing is unacceptable and God don't like it."

To convince me, he directed his youngest son to open his mouth revealing all the teeth God had taken. Yet, the voice in my mind said, *God will not take your teeth for swearing. God doesn't take teeth.*

At the age seven I had no proof of who was right, the people at church or the voice, but for some reason I trusted the voice in my mind more. In childhood, the things I experienced were accepted without question, but as I grew up and it became apparent that others did not share my experience, self-doubt and denial blossomed.

My family stopped attending church when my parents separated and later divorced. My mother disliked it and regarded most of the congregation as "busybodies and do-gooders." She often felt judged by fellow attendees.

"Do-gooders," she would mutter after church, "I wish they would keep their do-gooder opinions to themselves."

In contrast, I looked forward to Sundays when I was a child. I would search the bright ceiling of the sanctuary, following the light and imaging I was God's special friend with a secret shared only between us.

Even before I saw the flying beam on the ceiling of the chapel, I'd experienced a light vision. My sister Maggie and I were close from a young age. We shared a room together where we slept side- by- side in a double bed.

Most nights we would snuggle together, our nightgowns tangled among our spindly legs, whispering secrets and giggling in the dark.

One night, when I was five, I saw a soft light hovering above my sister. The light had a soft golden glow and felt like music which resonated in my body rather than in my ears—a melodious vibration that made my body buzz. I gazed intently at the light and was not afraid. Instead, I was lulled to sleep.

From that night on, I looked for the light so that I could relax and fall asleep. On one occasion, I reached up as far as I could to touch the magical glow while Maggie slept, but my hand felt only air. The light hovered over Maggie for several years and occasionally I would even catch a glimpse of it during the day, but I saw it best at night. I always felt closer to my sister while the light was there and yet I never mentioned its presence. Only years later would I understand that the beautiful glow above my older sister was an angel.

～

THE YEAR that I saw the light was the same year that my parents learned that Maggie had a rare disease called Hand- Schuller- Christian, commonly fatal. Our parents kept the news from us, but Maggie sensed something was wrong. She had a recurring nightmare,

"I'm dead," she'd whisper, "and they put me in a coffin and keep me in the garage all by myself until Christmas. That's the only day they wake me up and let me out."

Fear radiated from her tear-filled eyes. Her lips would part revealing thick nighttime spit that created gummy strings inside her mouth as she sucked in air and cried, "I don't want to be dead in the garage." Her breath was hot against my face and filled with the smells of sleep.

"Will you tickle my back till I fall back to sleep?" she would ask through tears.

I would then dance my fingers across her skin until sleep found us both again. By some miracle, the disease went into remission by the time Maggie was nine. Before that, she suffered years of experimental drug treatments that rendered her fat and bloated one year and emaciated the next. She underwent surgery to remove a tumor caused by the disease, yet the doctors predicted more. Yet for some reason Maggie was given reprieve from this terrible illness. She simply went into remission, freeing her from further suffering and possible death.

It's likely that you or someone you know has had an angelic encounter. Hundreds of thousands of people report seeing an angel or having experienced an interaction with what they describe as "angelic intervention." Some claim their life, or the life of someone they love, was saved by our angelic brethren. There are literally countless blogs, articles and books devoted to the subject, from the beginning of documented literature. I personally know dozens of people who claim an angelic experience. I eventually came to understand that the beaming light above Maggie was an angel there to protect and spare her.

The angel and flying lights in church weren't the only things I saw that others did not. I had a childhood friend named Angela who lived down the street in an old, white, clapboard house. We spent one summer playing together nearly every day. Angela had stringy, light brown hair that always had a snarl in the back like it was never combed. She was so skinny that she reminded me of Olive Oyl from the Popeye cartoon.

One afternoon as we played, we ran into her house, our hands clutched together in girlish delight. The air inside was cool and the rooms were small and completely separate from one another, walled off like a house of tiny boxes. I could smell the faint scent of flowers, although, I never found them.

I loved the gauzy mauve curtains that hung in the front room window, delicately tied back at each side with a pretty bow just like in a catalog. A giant wooden cabinet that dominated the dining room was filled with tiny porcelain figurines of couples dancing and delicate women in big hats.

Angela held my hand, pulling me like a mother elephant through the house. We passed a small parlor and I saw an old woman sitting rigidly in a chair facing the backyard near the window. She didn't speak or acknowledge us as we ran noisily past.

Her hair was white and her lips were pursed in discontent. Throughout the day, each time we went inside to play, the old woman sat in the chair, never smiling or looking in our direction and I wondered why. I assumed she was Angela's grandmother. After seeing her several times, I finally asked, "Is that your Grandma who's always in that chair?" We were poised at the top of the stairs, my finger pointed down at the woman.

Angela turned to look at me, wrinkled her nose and shrugged, "Huh?"

Somehow, I knew better than to ask again. I saw the woman plain as day, but Angela clearly did not. It was the first time I remember confirming that I saw what others didn't.

Increasingly, I began to notice that people did not see the things I saw, and although I wondered why, I never had the courage to ask anyone.

It was around the same time period that I began to notice an energy light that hovered around people. I would later learn the light was commonly called an aura, or electromagnetic field. But at the time I simply knew them as lights that people had. Some of the lights were easier to see than others. The lights had patterns in them and were different depending on the individual. The first time I recall noticing the light around my mother, she was in a fury.

My mother was beautiful, with coal black hair which she would later dye blonde and blue eyes that looked like shattered glass when she was angry. She could cripple me with one look.

I was six the first time I saw the rage that surrounded her body. My mother's light moved in an arc, with razor-like edges. I was rounded up along with my three sisters and marched into the hot, airless garage where we stood like soldiers lined up by age. My mother bent down, riffling through the contents of the standing freezer like a madwoman, her shorts exposing the fleshy meat of her thighs.

"Where is the damn Cool Whip?" she shrieked, as thick clouds of cold air puffed around her. My oldest sister, Karina, was first in line. "Did you eat the Cool Whip?" my mother bellowed.

"No, ma'am," Karina said, her voice trembling. "I haven't been here all day."

"Don't get smart with me, young lady," my mother warned. "I'll knock that smirk right off your face." She turned. "Isla," she snarled, "Did you eat the Cool Whip?"

Isla's blue eyes widened with fear. "No ma'am," she whispered. Isla's white, bloodless fingertips were wrapped in rubber bands, evidence of the bad habit she had for collecting them from random sidewalks.

Mom stepped closer to her. "Don't you lie to me missy. Someone damn sure ate it and I will find out who and then I'm going to kick your little butt's for lying to me."

She pointed a wooden spoon down the line at each one of us. Turning to Maggie, she asked her question again. Maggie too denied eating the Cool Whip. My mother's temper boomed.

"Now you listen to me, dammit! I will beat the snot out each one of you until whoever did this admits it."

My stomach pumped in and out in quick succession in a nervous habit under my tee shirt.

"Nita, did you eat the Cool Whip?"

"No, ma'am," I squeaked, tears already slipping down my cheeks.

"That's it!" she screamed and her hands flew into the air in a tantrum. "Nobody ate it? Fine, Nita, you're first!" she snarled, snatching me by the arm and holding me tight.

"Noooo," I cried, "I didn't do it. No, Mom, please."

The wooden spoon stung the back of my thighs and butt as she swung wildly. I danced around, my free arm swinging behind me hoping to ward off the blows. Before each spanking, she asked the question again and again. With each "No, ma'am," the spoon landed anew.

Each of us took the punishment until it was Karina' s turn.

"I did it! I ate the Cool Whip," Karina screamed, hoping to escape the beating with a lie.

But it was too late and Karina, like the rest of us, got what was coming.

It was during this incident that I first realized that the light surrounding my mother moved in patterns. It was her anger dancing, cutting and sharp.

Ultimately, I would notice that all living things had a pattern or light specific only to them, much like a thumbprint. The patterns revealed information about who that person was and what might be occurring in their life. I would learn over time to tune into these vibrations and read the field of energy like the map of a person's inner self.

From a young age my sister Isla saw the energy too, but not around people. Instead she could commune with animals,

listening to them and feeling their special energy. I remember one afternoon, not long after the Cool Whip episode, our parents took us on a rare family outing to the Japanese Tea Gardens in San Francisco's Golden Gate Park.

Before we left the car, our mother turned to the back seat giving stern directives for the day.

"Remember to hold hands at all times until we reach the park. Karina, you hold Isla's hand and Maggie, you and Nita hold hands. Do not talk to strangers under any circumstance, do you understand?" She asked.

"Yes, ma'am," we said in unison.

"And I will only tell you one time to do something," she said staring us down. "Do I make myself clear?"

"Yes, ma'am."

"Isla, don't let me catch you picking up any damn gum. And you girls better behave," she warned pointing her finger at us. We nodded our heads in agreement.

We were not allowed to chew gum at home so Isla would find discarded gum on the sidewalk, plucking it from the ground and popping the already chewed wad into her mouth. Our mother railed at Isla when she did this screaming, "You'll get worms, Isla! That is a disgusting habit!"

That summer my mother searched Isla, myself for worms more than once. The hunt for the tiny worms began at night, and consisted of our mother bending us over without our panties in a darkened room. She'd spread our bare cheeks and shine a flashlight on our exposed bums. This was a traumatic event, always starting and ending in tears. She was an R.N. working at a doctor's office causing her to be hyper-vigilant about such things.

The day at the tea gardens we ran around screeching with delight, racing down the tiny winding paths and curved bridges that went over and alongside of a stream filled with giant koi-fish.

I spotted Isla squatting at the edge of the water, watching intently as the fish swam languidly past. I sidled up next to her to see what was so intriguing and Isla said, "Look at that fish. He's the happiest fish in there."

"But how do you know?" I'd asked looking into her wide blue eyes.

"Because he told me so. And he's shinier than the others. It means he's the happiest, see?" she said pointing at the fish.

I saw a golden fish with beautiful black spots and shiny skin that reflected the sun, but he looked like all the others who swam past.

As I gazed at the fish in the gurgling stream, Isla nudged me and said in a whisper, "Look, I have something for you." She opened her sweaty palm and there in the middle of it was a pale green morsel of previously chewed gum.

"Here," she offered. "It's for you."

I snatched the sticky wad and plopped it happily into my mouth. "Thanks, Isla!"

"Don't let mom see or she'll give you the worms." Isla warned.

An intensely private person, my mother never offered insight into her past. As an adult, I realized that she suffered from low self-esteem, self-loathing, and a general inability to cope with children.

She had a photo album that was black with gold lettering and read: "PORTRAITS of Caroline Penry." The large, hardcover book was filled with 12x10 black-and-white photographs of herself from infancy to twenty-one years old. Among the images was a picture of her mother clad in shimmering sequins with a matching headband and veil. I was fascinated with the album the beautiful photos showing elegant poses, fancy clothes, and ornate jewelry. But most importantly, they provided the only window into my mother's past.

One afternoon I eagerly opened the book, pointed to photos and asked my mother,

"Is this you?" "Yes," she replied.

Then I reached a photo of a smiling woman who was grossly fat. I thought the woman looked imminently sad and not at all like my mother. I asked, "Who is this?"

She snatched the album from my hands and slammed it shut. "Put this godforsaken thing away before you ruin it," she snapped.

Years later I would discover that the fat girl in the album was my mother at age fourteen. In her youth, she struggled mightily

with her weight, reaching what we label today as "morbid obesity." My mother struggled with that image of herself. It was a reminder of a sad, dysfunctional, childhood that held no joy.

She grew up in a wealthy suburb with both money and opportunity. She was a debutant and had a "coming out party," a fairytale event in my mind. Her family had domestic staff that cooked, cleaned, and tended the grounds, working daily at her large, white-washed home, quiet on a stately street.

She was estranged from her family. Later, when our grandmother committed suicide, three years would pass after her death before my mother even found out. She also had an older sister, who I knew only from photos, and a half-brother too with Down syndrome who lived in an institution. She rarely spoke of her family at all.

Years later my mother explained to me why she married our father. "I never loved him," she said. "When I got pregnant with

Karina, my father forced me to marry her father. But he was abusive. I divorced him in less than a year and moved back home. It was like a living in hell."

Both of my parents were alcoholics" she continued. "I hated them. There was no love in that house. I married Dell, to get away and make them angry. They disowned me, cut me out of their wills for marrying beneath my status, but I didn't care. They could keep their filthy money. He was my ticket out. When we met, your father was uneducated and poor with no future. I drug him through flight school. If not for me, he would never have gone anywhere in life."

This would be the only time my mother spoke of her past to me.

My father, Dell, came from extreme poverty, a fact that was often whispered in conversation. My mother would say, "That man was dirt poor and lucky he had shoes on his feet."

Growing up in poverty defined my father. He had a lifelong fear of never having enough.

"That poor man," I heard my mother say into the phone receiver one night while she stood at the sink rinsing dishes. "He never got over his piece-of-filth father who left him standing by the gate from morning till night waiting with a fishing pole and bucket for a fishing trip he would never go on. He didn't give a damn about Dell and everyone knew it."

Yet, gifted with a high IQ, my father would fly planes and captain boats for a living. I thought my father was handsome and charismatic, with deep blue eyes and blond hair. When I was told that I looked just like him, I swelled with pride. He was rarely home, and I yearned for his attention and affection.

A few weeks before my mother left my father for good, he sat alone in our living room. The song, "Tiny Bubbles," rang out on the stereo speakers. The album cover, propped in front of one speaker, featured a smiling, brown-skinned man sporting a flowered necklace. I climbed into his lap, breathing in the smell of cigarettes and Old Spice, feeling the hum of his chest while he sang along to his favorite song. I sang too, having memorized all the words.

He held me close, bumping his knee to the song's beat making me bounce up and down. I could feel his love in the warmth and squeeze of his hands. I don't ever remember sitting in my mother's lap or hearing whispers of love. He was perfect in my eyes, and I wished I could stay that way forever.

I left for school one morning, everything completely normal. But as I neared my house that afternoon, I saw the giant orange moving van in our driveway. I walked through the door, arms filled with books. Everyone was busy running in different directions. Boxes were scattered throughout the house, and upon seeing me, my mother barked, "Nita, go to your room and pack your things."

"But why. Where are we going?" I asked, puzzled. "Do as you're told, dammit. Now get going!" Panic seized me.

When I got to the room I shared with Maggie, she was filling a box with clothes.

"Why are we leaving?" I asked, tears threatening.

Before she could answer, my oldest sister, Karina, stood in the doorway and said, "You better stop sniveling and hurry up."

"But where's Daddy?" I asked, now openly crying.

"He's not coming," she said. "Mom's leaving him." And with that Karina turned and was gone.

When my mother left my father, he was working as a flight engineer for a commercial airline. As it happened, he wasn't due home for a couple of days, but my mother had "a feeling" and called the flight desk to inquire as to his whereabouts. The response, "Oh Dell, well he left yesterday. His wife and son picked him up." It was a shocking revelation. My father had a secret family living in another state.

My mother promptly left him and never looked back.

We drove for almost three days, eventually arriving in California. Mother was giddy as we crested a hill with a large sign at the side of the road that read, "Welcome to California: The Sunshine State." This marked the beginning of a surge in my intuitive ability.

THE BOY ABANDONED

When the boy awoke, he was alone in a strange room. A wet heat suffocated him. The distant bellow of a cow mooing and the squawking of chickens brought the memories back. His parents had abandoned him. Threw him away like trash. Shipped him off.

The boy had been in constant trouble and although only nine years old, he would sneak out at night and steal from stores, angry, defiant, not caring if he got caught, which he frequently did. Now, as a result he was miles away on a desolate farm living with an aunt and uncle he did not know.

The bedroom door opened and his uncle poked his head in, "It's time ya git up buddy and git a start on chores now. This is how we do it 'round here. Ain't no trouble for ya ta git up to. Let's git a move on."

It took several months for the boy to accept his new life, which was hard at first. He cried at night feeling isolated and alone. His aunt and uncle didn't have children of their own and seemed happy to have the boy with them. Unlike his parents, they were patient and kind. He grew to love them and he found comfort in working on the farm. He slowly began to forget the stinking, rot of his father and after two years of his new life the boy was happy and felt loved.

One morning before the sun rose, he hurried to the barn to check on the cat who'd just had kittens. Kneeling in the soft dirt he scooped up the tiny mewing babies and nuzzled his face in their silky fur. "It's gonna be a good day," he said to the purring mother cat. "Don't look like it'll be too hot." Putting the kittens down he said, "I'll be back later."

The boy worked steadily, sweating in the sun when his uncle called to him from across the field, "Git in the truck will ya and move it back from them barn doors. We got hay comin. Keys is in it."

The boy jumped in the cab and twisted backwards so he could see behind him. As he reversed the old truck he felt his tire roll over something. He turned and looked through the windshield shading his eyes from the glare of the sun. There, squirming in the dirt was the mother cat.

"Nooo! Oh, buddy! I didn't see ya."

The boy bolted from the cab and ran to the spot where she now lay still. He lifted her up and held her close. Tiny rivulets of blood seeped from her nose. Tears coursed down his cheeks, "I'm so sorry," he cried into the animal's fur. The boy gripped her neck and twisted, releasing her from suffering. His sense of loss was enormous and the boy was sick with it for days, unable to leave his bed.

Only a week later his mother called and said, "Send the youngin home."

The boy's heart broke even more. He was happy with his aunt and uncle on the farm, but he was powerless. He went home, bitter and enraged. He would never forget how his parents threw him away so easily just two years ago, no sir, he would never forget.

3

I gave my first psychic reading at the age of eight. I had no idea what I was doing. It was spontaneous and I hadn't known I could do it until the moment it occurred.

It happened while spending time with a new acquaintance, an adult. Her name was Angie and she lived with her husband and toddler in the neighborhood where we'd just moved.

We sat together at her kitchen table. An oscillating fan on the floor blew the bangs from my sticky forehead. My elbows were planted firmly atop the round table, which was covered with dominoes. My chin rested nicely in sweaty palms while my fingertips played my bottom lip like a bass drum as I listened intently to Angie explain the rules of the game again.

"Sammy, stop that now," Angie yelled, interrupting her instructions.

Her son sat spread eagle on the floor just a few feet away in a circle of toys. Sam spit the matchbox car from his slobbering mouth and smiled a single toothed grin at his mother.

How we met is vague in my memory, but in my loneliness after our hurried move I somehow ended up at her house every day. I will forever feel like she was my first real friend. We developed a strong and unique bond. Our iced tea glasses sweated wet rings onto the multicolored coasters beneath them and Angie continued to review the rules.

"Now remember," she said, "you can only pick seven the first time, and if you get one with the same amount of dots on each end, it's a double and those are good."

She smiled and I admired her dewy skin and hazel eyes. Her hair was blade-straight and fell like a thick, black shade to her shoulders.

"Why don't you go first this time," she said as she winked at me.

"Okay," I eagerly agreed.

My thumb caressed the smooth back of the ebony domino and I placed each one carefully on the tray in front of me. We played for a while when out of the blue Angie said,

"I don't know why I got married. I don't know what I was thinking."

She exhaled her pent-up breath and gazed at her son playing on the floor.

I heard a voice in my head that said, Yes you do. You wanted him to love you so you felt worthy even though you didn't love him. He supports what you believe about yourself.

Without thinking I repeated the information although it was well beyond my understanding. Angie said nothing as she stared at me, her lips parted as if she were going to speak. I felt her astonishment float like an invisible secret in the air between us and I regretted what I had said even as the words slipped from my memory. I *knew* that what the voice had said was a hidden truth that only she comprehended.

I sat at her kitchen table and I *knew* she didn't love her husband and I *knew* he had hurt her in ways I could feel, but not understand. I felt the essence that was him. I saw in my mind's eye his curly hair and boyish smile. I felt his stern and unbending, demeanor, although I had never met him.

"My god," she breathed, "you are only a child. How can you know this stuff?"

Angie then asked me questions. The answers channeled through me, in the form of the voice, accompanied with the *knowing*. She fixed me with her hazel eyes and said, "No one will believe me. I can't tell anyone what you say. They'll think I'm crazy." She reached over and squeezed my hand. In that moment I felt so worthy and loved.

I didn't know how I knew the things that I did, but I wanted her to like me and be my friend. I felt special providing her with what seemed like valuable information. It was the first time I felt important. That was how it started, and from then on when I visited, that was what we did-we played dominoes and Angie talked to the voice.

It was simple, really. I heard a voice in my mind and when I repeated what I heard, the listener found remarkable insight into issues or events I couldn't possibly know. The information I received was well beyond my understanding and I had no clear recall of what I said even moments after I spoke the words. That fact is still true today.

After about a month, I arrived home one afternoon and my mother asked, "What are you doing at that woman's house every day?"

"She's my friend," I replied. "We play dominoes and drink iced tea and stuff. She's my friend," I repeated defensively.

My mother stared at me, her eyes fleecing me, searching for the truth.

"It is not normal for a grown woman to make friends with an eight-year-old," she replied.

But why not? I thought. "She likes me," I said, "and we're friends."

"She must be terribly lonely," my mother commented.

"No," I said, "We're friends. I help her with Sam and we talk about stuff."

My mother stiffened, "What stuff?" she asked.

"I don't know, just stuff," I said as I shrugged. "Her husband is probably having an affair," I blurted out, though we'd never talked about that and I didn't understand where it came from.

"Did she tell you this?" my mother questioned.

"No. I just know," I responded and immediately realizing my mistake. What came next was devastating for me.

"You are not to go to that woman's house again. I mean it, young lady. That relationship is inappropriate," my mother said.

Tears welled up and my throat felt like I swallowed a popsicle. "But she's my friend," I croaked. "We play dominoes. Mom, pleeease."

But my pleading got me nowhere, and that was the end of it. No further discussion. I ran down the hall and hurled myself on the bed crying. *I hate you, I just hate you*, I screamed in my mind.

A month later we moved across town to a small apartment complex. I never had the chance to say goodbye to my only friend.

I couldn't have known that my mother was trying to protect me from information she felt I shouldn't have. Years later, she would tell me that she didn't acknowledge how strong the Clairs were within me because my *knowing* and comments made her uncomfortable.

Around this same time, I began to see *pictures* or visions behind my eyes—or at least that was the best way I knew how to describe them. Receiving pictures was like participating in and observing a three-dimensional movie simultaneously. My *pictures* brought insight and ambiguity, puzzles and explanation. Ultimately, they molded the person I would become.

When the *pictures* came, I was held captive. They happened spontaneously and could show anything. Seconds before they began, everything stopped. Sight, sound, and senses were suspended in the present moment and a channel opened through which the images entered. The experience was not like a seizure that paralyzes, but rather it was a shift in attention. While observing the *pictures,* I experienced fully the feelings, thoughts, smells, sounds, and senses of the people I saw.

I called them "*pictures,*" but others might say "prophetic visions" or "psychic visions" to describe the same thing. I didn't know why I received *pictures* about certain things and not others.

One Saturday morning, not long after we moved from Angie's neighborhood, I sat perched on the cold cement steps that led to the second floor where we lived. Bent nearly in half, my cheeks planted firmly between my scabby knees, I peered down between the steps at a delicate spider web that hung there. The vision began.

Two women were sitting at a kitchen table talking and smoking. Their cigarettes dangled with ash, their breath hot with coffee, and their hearts were heavy with judgment. As this scene became clear to me, it was like I was an invisible ghost floating in the room. I knew what they felt and thought like we were all connected—like we were one.

"Can you believe it!? She is barely twenty one, not married, and on her second baby!"

Somehow, I knew this woman's name was Tanya. She wore cutoff jeans whose fuzzy trimmed threads circled her perfectly smooth and lightly tanned thighs. She had the long face of a horse. Tanya snorted, "My God. My brothers would kill me!" She leaned her slender body forward and widened her pale brown eyes to exaggerate her point. "I mean they would kill me *after* they killed him of course."

Unfolding her long legs, she pushed back from the table, made her way to the sink, and poured the coffee down the drain. The small, dingy kitchen had sticky counters stacked with dirty dishes.

Holly, the other woman at the round table, lifted a cigarette to her lips, pulled hard, and blew smoke towards the ceiling as she considered her response. "She has always been trash. Always will be, I guess."

Holly was petite with delicate features and had the exotic look of a beauty queen. She wore a homemade halter-top in the shape of a kerchief that was tied so tightly at her neck and back that it burrowed into her soft skin, leaving deep marks from the weight of her surprisingly large bosoms.

Holly continued, "I mean, I didn't even have sex until I was nineteen, and even then Billy and I had already been together, what, two years?" Holly held up her tiny hand and showed two fingers, a testament to her virtue. Crushing her cigarette, she leaned back.

At that moment I felt her sweaty shoulder stick to the plastic chair.

She took a sip of coffee, now cold, made a face and glanced proudly into her living room. A tattered green floral couch and cheap knickknacks with dust covered neglect filled the room.

Holly was lying about her sexual past. She told the truth about her relationship with Billy, but she had omitted the fact that she lost her virginity at age fourteen in a dark musty room to someone else, which no one knew about, including Billy. We all have our secrets.

As the women continued to gossip, I knew they were talking about me, and although they were not my friends, I knew they were from somewhere in my life that was waiting. I lost all sense of time as the 3-D movie unfolded in my mind. I accepted what I saw without question or judgment. I didn't fully grasp the meaning of what I had witnessed. Yet, like any kid I quickly dismissed the event and returned to bitter thoughts about my mother with whom I was still very angry. It wasn't long after that day that the phone calls started between my parents. My mother screamed into the phone,

"If you weren't such a selfish prick, none of this would have happened. Oh c'mon, Dell, you don't give a shit about these girls."

The accusations and arguments went on for months until it was finally decided that Isla, Maggie, and I would spend the summer with our father and his "other" wife, Milda. My eldest sister, Karina, whose father was from my mother's previous marriage, did not have to go live with Dell.

At the end of the summer, Isla and Maggie returned home, while I chose to stay with my father.

"You'll be sorry," Maggie warned as she packed her suitcase. "You're an idiot," she spat.

But I was delighted to live with my father, and practically floated on air that first week. There would be no competition for his love from my sisters. Milda had a son from a previous marriage named Dickey. He was two years older than me—the son my father always wanted.

But I felt no jealousy. Unlike Dickey, I was my father's real child and, in my mind, his favorite. What I couldn't have known when I made the decision to stay, was the terrible physical abuse I would receive over the next several years. Or that my father would do nothing to protect me from it.

Milda was short and stout with large brown eyes and black hair teased and sprayed which she wore like a helmet. She was obsessed with cleanliness. Her home always had the unmistakable smell of Pine-sol on its gleaming floors. The first night as a new family, Milda prepared crispy fried chicken, mashed potatoes and homemade biscuits with gravy for dinner. The delicious smells permeated the air and the kitchen window fogged with condensation wafting up from the stove.

I sat at the table for four feeling pride that the cheap Kmart china matched. We passed hot plates of food to one another like a real family and Milda was radiant at the dinner table, glowing with happiness.

She looked directly at me and smiled as she spoke, "I ain't ever had a daughter and I always wanted one. I'm so glad it's gonna be you. This weekend, we can go shopping and buy some new clothes and shoes. Would you like that, honey?"

I was so happy I could burst as I eagerly nodded my head. *Who wouldn't be happy? This is fantastic*, I thought. I was going to be like a real princess. What my eyes saw in Milda as happiness, was actually the glow of alcohol.

We dug into our food and my father said, "This is just the best fried chicken I think I ever had." He looked up at Milda, smiling with greasy lips, and winked.

I scooped my spoon into my mashed potatoes smothered in Southern gravy, wrinkling my nose as I forced myself to swallow. Instead of using milk to thicken and sweeten the gravy, Milda had used water from the boiled potatoes. Unaccustomed to the taste of the watery soup, my displeasure was impossible to hide. I avoided the potatoes and gravy completely. As she watched, Milda's agitation inflated to dangerous levels. Her mood and expression changed shifting her energetic field instantly.

She hissed, "What's the matter, missy? You don't like my gravy?"

The glow on her face, was replaced with a belligerent sneer. Her energy frightened me. Shaking my head back and forth I whispered, "No, ma'am."

Leaning in toward me, she snapped, "Why not? Is it because I don't use milk like her highness?" she taunted, referring to my mother, whom she hated.

Her finger made a curly cue in the air as she spoke. A clear view of Milda's silver fillings shone in her mouth as she exaggerated the words "her highness" and the sharp smell of alcohol washed over me. The chair scraped loudly as Milda stood up from the table, the color rising in her cheeks.

Rigid with fear, my stomach clenched in response.

Milda's face was inches from mine as she slurred, "In my house you don't get to turn your nose up, you hear me?!"

My father and stepbrother sat mute, watching the event unfold.

"But I don't like it," I whined, tears spilling over.

In an instant, Milda slapped the side of my head three or four times. I'd never been slapped before. Her warm palm against my face was shocking. It took a moment to even register what was happening. She grabbed a handful of my hair, snatched the spoon from my hand, and began forcing mashed potatoes and gravy into my mouth.

"Open your mouth!" she screamed.

Potatoes and gravy landed with wet thumps on my bare thighs. I gagged on the food, tears, and snot and vomited as Milda slapped my head again and again, screaming words I couldn't hear. Still holding a fist full of hair, she rattled my head back and forth.

I had no recollection of getting cleaned up and going to bed. Lying in the dark, I sucked in air and tried desperately to hold back tears. With each heartbeat the back of my head throbbed in complaint.

My father never intervened and, in my mind, there was no question that I was at fault. *Why couldn't I just eat the gravy?* I thought, as I lay in the darkness, worried and fearful. Suddenly, harsh yellow light spilled into the room as the door opened. Milda stumbled to the bed crying openly.

"I'm so sorry honey," she hiccupped. Her emotion rushed toward me like a giant wave. "You're my daughter now and I'm sorry honey. I love you. I really do."

She said all these things as she held me. We both cried and I patted her back to comfort her. I felt responsible for her tears. Drunk and slurring, she held my face between her hands and said, "Don't you ever spit out my food again. You hear me? I am a right good cook and everyone likes my cooking. Everyone."

"Ok-k-kay, I won't. I' m s-s-s-s- orry."

A high, keening whine left my throat as sobbing took hold and I bowed my head in shame. I felt awful for my behavior. The beating would be the first of physical abuse that I would endure for the next year and a half until my sister; Maggie, would come rescue me.

My father never spoke of the incident. It was only one of many times I felt abandoned by him.

For the rest of his life, our father would put the woman he was married to first, and his children would fit where they fit. Initially, this behavior caused me pain and confusion. I believed that I was less important to him. Ultimately, though, I have come to see it was my father's gift to me. Because of him, I had to find self-worth from within. I had to discover that I was worth loving despite my father's inability to show me. I found that receiving love was a choice I could make. It had nothing to do with who my father loved- a powerful lesson that only made me stronger.

The following weekend we went camping by a lake. I'd never camped or gone anywhere overnight as a family, and I was silly with excitement.

The water was cold and my skin prickled with goose bumps. I couldn't force the grin from my face even as I danced on slippery stones, slowly going deeper into the lake though I knew I shouldn't. I didn't know how to swim and wore no life vest.

The last thing I saw before slipping beneath the water's edge were shining pinpoints across the lake's surface. I could no longer feel the bottom and panic seized me. Spastically my arms and legs moved in opposite directions. The murky water became colder as I sunk and water filled my ears. I could only hear the noise of my drumming heart.

Something suddenly squeezed my ribcage. Air bubbles, carrying the last of my breath, floated upward seconds before my face broke the surface of the water. I sucked a mixture of water and air gagging on both.

I lay on my side in a spasm of coughing and choking. The sharp edges of tiny rocks pricked my skin, my swimsuit lodged between my buttocks.

"That's it child, get it out, you'll be just fine," came the unfamiliar voice of a woman whose cold, wet hand slapped my back.

Someone screamed, "Dell! You better get over here!"

"Good god almighty" my father said kneeling at my side. "What in the hell happened? I turn my back for one minute!" he lied.

Neither my father nor Milda sat with the other adults on the lake's rocky shore watching their children play.

The woman said, "Just leave her with me. I'll be here all day with my daughter. I'll watch them both."

"I sure do appreciate that. I turned my back for one minute..."

"Don't you worry now. We've all had accidents. I'll see to her."

"Well thank ya now, a, what was your name?"

"Helen. I'm Helen and this is Deanna. She's mine. Dee is blind but she plays like she isn't, don't ya, Dee."

A young girl with wet, curly hair, and a missing front tooth grinned. Her left eye, as blue as the sky, wandered in its socket.

"Yes ma'am," she said.

Deanna and I became fast friends and we played together the rest of the day.

At dusk she and her mom went to their campsite and I headed to ours. I hadn't seen anyone for hours and there was no one in our camper. My skin burned red from the sun, and I shivered as I walked toward the scent of burgers on an open fire. My stomach roared with hunger.

"Oh-oh my god. Ahhh! Ahhhh!" I heard screaming and followed the sound.

A camper, its door opened wide, spilled dim light down the metal steps. Inside Milda lay on the banquette screaming and thrashing, her black hair piece flailing as she jerked and kicked wildly into the air. She struggled to land punches on the back of a woman who was holding her down.

"Why! Why does everyone leave me? I hate him. I hate that bastard! He's always leavin me behind!" She wailed.

"I know it, honey. I know it. Just let it out Milda. Let it out now."

I stood mesmerized. I'd never seen an adult have a tantrum. I was too young to understand that not only was Milda drunk, she was coming undone.

She continued to scream, but my attention was drawn to the cloud of energy above her. I was accosted with the *knowing*. The cloud held all of Milda's sadness, rage, and desperation. It held the dark bruises of her body's memory.

I had no frame of reference for the word "abuse" but I felt it there. In my mind's eye I saw a man. He was huge with dark eyes and slicked-back hair. He was mean and hateful and somehow, I *knew* he was connected to her.

I felt tightness in my chest and a compassion for Milda. I *knew* she was lost in a fog of suffering and pain. I *knew* she would never find her way out. I also *knew* that was just the way it would always be for Milda.

Only nine years old, what I saw and what I *knew* that day would never leave me.

THE BOY—A FATHER'S LEGACY

The boy, back at home entered middle school. He no longer feared his father. His fear turned to hatred. He was resentful that his mother obediently went to bed with him every night.

The boy's father was still a drunk, coming home cursing and stinking of booze. He staggered blindly through the house, knocking over lamps and breaking knick-knacks in his path of drunken cruelty.

When the boy returned home from the farm, he had a little brother, whom he loved instantly and protected no matter the cost. Several years had passed now since the boy had been nearly suffocated in the trunk. The first chance he got, he emptied the chest, discarding it in a vacant lot to prevent his little brother from the same fate.

For as long as the boy could remember, his mother had worked as an aide at a nursing home. Most days, she came home wrung out. Yet, she still cooked dinner and waited on her husband hand- and-foot, angering the boy further.

One afternoon in an alcoholic haze, his father became convinced his wife was cheating on him. He sat in the stifling heat, of his truck's cab, waiting for her to finish work. He stuffed tobacco into his bottom lip and watched through bloodshot eyes.

I'll show her. I'll follow her and catch her red handed, he thought as he spit bitter, brown juice out the open window.

∽

His wife, Bernadette, rubbed her lower back to relieve the ache that throbbed there. She was grateful her long shift was nearly finished. She smiled when her friend, Edie sidled up next to her, "Oh gal, aren't you glad we can call it a day? Whew, I am beat," Edie said, blowing her short bangs from her forehead.

Bernadette lifted her pencil-thin eyebrows carefully drawn over her sky-blue eyes and said, "You can say that again, sister. What in tarnation was I thinking when I agreed to a shift that starts at five a.m.?"

The women stood at the nurse's station and filled out their paper work, continuing the small talk.

"Oh, say Edie, do you still need a ride home? Ain't a problem for me. I can drop you, but I gotta get some gas first. That sound good?"

"You know, that would be just great if you don't mind, hon. I know you need to get home to your boys."

"Listen, I'll run get my purse and meet you at the car. I'm just around back," Bernadette said as she walked away.

"Okay, hon, thanks," Edie said focusing on her reports. Although the air that blew through the car windows was warm,

it released the pent-up heat as the women drove to the gas station. Bernadette pulled her old car up to an available pump, put it in park, and turned toward her friend.

"I was thinkin'," Bernadette started. The next few seconds seemed like a dream. In slow motion, Edie fell toward Bernadette. In the same instant, Bernadette felt a burning in her chest. In utter shock, Bernadette saw the blood oozing from Edie's head. Dizziness overcame her as she reached for her friend. She heard a shot ring out and felt her shoulder explode.

The first bullet- the one that Bernadette hadn't heard- had burrowed through Edie's brain and lodged itself in her own chest.

Edie died instantly and Bernadette would lose a lung in surgery later. Just before she lost consciousness, she saw her husband stumbling toward her, a gun in his hand.

The man did his best to stand straight. *I done showed them, cheatin' has consequences.* Bleary eyed and drunk, he bent over to peer inside the car. He could hear people screaming and running, like cockroaches in the light, but he didn't care.

~

Bernadette was slumped forward behind the steering wheel. The man shuffled to the open passenger window and witnessed his handiwork. Satisfaction rushed through him as he thought, *Hotdam! I got the cheatin' bastard too.* A smile began to curl his slick, wet lips just as police cars roared in from four directions.

Suddenly, he had a realization cut through his drunken, stupor. He stumbled backwards trying to reconcile his thoughts. *Why does this turkey have tits?* he pondered, as the cop nearest him screamed, "Drop your weapon!"

4

The clashing of cymbals exploded in my ears. My neck snapped back and forth like a rubber hose as bloody snot oozed over my lips. I remember how it felt inside more than how it hurt. The sting of shame burned deep within long after the marks had faded away.

Milda's beatings had become regular, occurring countless times a month now. I was beaten for not cleaning the floor around the bottom of the toilet. I was beaten for having the wrong expression. Sometimes a simple shrug of shoulders followed by an, "I don't know" garnered a solid slap across the face or a punch in the ribs. At some point during this period of abuse I began leaving my body and observing the traumatic events from above the fray, like a brazen voyeur.

My most vivid out-of-body experience happened a few weeks after we had gone camping. I spontaneously left my body and observed the painful experience with an odd sense of understanding that was the *knowing*.

The sky was pale and cloudless, a warning of heat and humidity to come. This would be my day. I was to have a formal introduction into Milda's family, and a picnic was planned to celebrate my arrival. Euphoria coursed through me like a drug. I craved recognition and praise in the same way others needed air to breathe.

I watched, giddy, as the first guests made their way down the long gravel drive. Dust billowed up from under the car's tires and hung in the hot Midwestern air. Picnic tables decorated with red- and-white checkered cloths were set up just beyond the covered patio.

My father's good looks and Southern charm shined as he welcomed each new arrival with a handshake or a hug, and I was bursting with pride as I met each family member. Milda had worked all morning preparing food and cleaning the house until everything was undeniably perfect. Dickey and I did our best to greet family members and guests. About an hour after the last car was parked and everyone was there, he and I stood outside adjacent to the horse corral.

"Hey Dickey, can we take the pony out so the little kids can ride?" I asked.

The pony belonged to our landlords who lived in the house next door. Dickey looked toward the barn, his cowboy hat pulled low to shade his eyes.

"Okay. I guess I could do that. I'll ask Dad."

Dickey came back with the pony and tied her to the fence while he saddled her. He hefted the saddle onto her back and pulled the cinch that ran under her belly to secure it. He then quickly lifted his knee and struck the pony hard in the stomach. The pony let out a whoosh of air like a burp.

"Ohh, Dickey!" I gasped at his blatant meanness.

Dickey muttered, "She holds her breath so she can make the saddle loose and cause the rider to fall. Don't you, you stinking mule," he said to her.

Sweat glistened thin and slick on his upper lip as he tightened the cinch again. Dickey had the same thickly lashed brown eyes as Milda. He played football and kept quiet most of the time. He had been beaten his whole life. "The best thing to do is just drop your head and let her go till she tires out," Dickey advised me weeks later. "Don't fight back. It just makes it last longer."

Dickey and I took turns that day leading the pony so the kids could ride. When we were finished, Dickey took charge.

"Give her to me and I'll tie her up," he huffed. I watched as he tied her bridle strap to a post.

"I'm just gonna leave her saddled in case someone wants to ride her later," he said.

Soon after, Milda marched toward me while I played on the swing set. Her face was tight with agitation. Her anger looked like sparklers on the fourth of July pulsing around her body. The pony had gotten loose and somehow it was my fault.

Milda shrieked. "How could you be so selfish, so stupid!?" Somebody could hit that horse and sue us. Your daddy and me could lose everything! What in the hell was you thinkin?!"

I froze.

Milda continued her tirade and moved closer. "You had better pray, your Daddy finds that horse, little girl," she threatened.

Then she slapped me so hard across the face, my ears rang. I lost my balance and fell to the ground. She yanked me across the pasture by my hair.

In those first few seconds, inside my ears, my hair sounded like grass being yanked from the ground by its roots. I stumbled and lurched like a rodeo clown and tears filled my eyes.

Milda dragged me into the dim barn that smelled of horse sweat, hay, and dirt. She spun me in a circle, and my head banged against the stall with a sharp sting. Her fists pounded my face and back. Handfuls of blonde hair flew out in all directions. Even though I knew she was hitting me, it felt as if she was beating someone else.

Suddenly, somehow, I was hovering outside of myself, watching the spit fly from Milda's mouth while she gritted her teeth and beat me. It was eerie.

I could see all around the barn. There were no edges or corners, no barriers to block what lay behind or beneath me.

A stench, like the smell of a trapped animal, filled the air. My stepmother's labored breath huffed out in clouds of hate. I could feel my heart banging against my ribs, but I was not inside my body as Milda hit me so hard her arms ached with fatigue. I *knew* what she felt, not just in her body, but in her mind too. I understood intuitively why she was losing control and yet, the nine-year-old child that I was, still experienced shock, shame, and immense fear. It was like the *knowing* belonged to someone else residing somewhere within me waiting for me to grow up.

Milda's rage blinded her. She was disconnected from her own actions, there was a vacancy within her. I could hear a high- pitched scream in her mind and just like that, I was back in my body.

Milda stopped beating me as abruptly as she started. A dozen shocked faces peered at me. No one spoke. No one moved. No one came to my aid. I thought the beating was acceptable and maybe somehow, I had it coming.

As everyone stared at my wild hair and the bloody snot that oozed from my nose, my skin burned, red with shame. *What would they think of me now?* I wondered as I sat bewildered in the dirt. My father was nowhere to be seen. I couldn't stop my tears and my body vibrated with revolt.

Milda's family members gathered around her attempting to calm an out of control and hysterical woman. While "out of my body" I experienced what Milda was feeling-confusion, fear, and explosive anger, and I *knew* in a weird way that she couldn't help herself. I remembered what I'd seen and felt while camping only the week before.

The *knowing* I experienced when I went "out of body" in the barn, was the same *knowing* I felt when seeing *pictures*. Yet, strangely the *knowing* that I felt during the readings with Angie differed slightly. When giving readings or repeating what I'd heard in my mind, I was unable to hear thoughts of the other person like I could when having *pictures* or being "out of body." Instead, I would experience their feelings. As a child, I understood the most basic aspect of the *knowing,* like what Milda felt. But the deeper message of why an event occurred at all was beyond my emotional scope. That part of the *knowing* would assist me in gaining insight into my past, and allow me to forgive years later in life.

I *knew* I wouldn't live with my father and Milda forever because I'd heard it from the voice. *"Don't worry,"* it said. *"You will be okay, it won't last forever. There is another life waiting for you."*

I believed what I heard and *knew*, but I had no words for it. Still, the beatings brought feelings of shame and remorse. I *knew* that what was happening to me was somehow preplanned and felt weirdly familiar. I was not able to explain or reconcile this information.

A year passed and somehow, I survived Milda's rage and violent outbursts. Maggie and Isla came to visit for the summer and Maggie stayed to live with us for a year. What occurred during this time created an unbreakable bond between us.

When they arrived with our father from the airport I squealed with delight!

"I'm so glad you're here," I cried, jumping up and down at the door.

"Me too, me too!" cried Maggie excitedly. Isla was not as happy to be there. She came because our mother made her.

"C'mon you guys, I'll show you our room." We ran like thunder down the hall.

"Look," I said, "You have your own beds and you can put all your stuff here." I pointed with pride to a white dresser.

We sat with our backs against my bed as Maggie and Isla showed me photos of all I had missed. Isla pulled a snapshot from the pile and held it under my nose. In it was a giant dog.

Isla said, "His name is Rory, and he's an Irish wolfhound. And he is the smartest and sweetest dog in the world. When he jumps up, I put his paws on my shoulders. See how big he is." she purred as she handed me a new photo. "And you can see what he's thinking by just looking into his eyes. You're so sweet aren't you," Isla said to the picture, planting a wet kiss on it.

Like the Koi fish years before, the Clairs manifested for her through animals. She assumed for most of her life that everyone could hear them and understand them like she did.

The happiness of our reunion was short-lived. Before two weeks had even passed Milda exploded at Isla. I was in the backyard when I heard shouting turn into shrieking. Ragged breath fogged the glass of the door as I cupped my hands at the sides of my face to peer inside.

Milda stood over Isla screaming and grabbing at her flailing arms. Isla lay in a tight fetal position on the floor, waving her arms trying to cover her head.

"Get up, get up off that floor! I'm not through with you," Milda shrieked.

"No! Don't hit me! Don't hit me!" Isla cried. Her face was so red, she looked sunburned. "No!" Isla screamed. "Stop it!"

Milda grabbed Isla easily by her long, golden hair and yanked it upwards while she threw punches with her free hand. Isla screamed, "Let go of me!" She kicked her legs like a wild horse.

Maggie ran to the phone and called the police as I slipped inside through the glass slider. Ten minutes later there was a knock at the front door. A police officer stood alone on the front stoop. He bent at the waist drawing my attention to his smooth brown eyes. "Are you alright, missy?" The officer asked.

Screams and curses rang out and tumbled onto the porch. "Yes," I squeaked through my tears.

In one motion, the officer gently pushed me aside and went in the house. I ran crying to my room, diving on my bed while the fighting escalated. The soft, cotton quilt was cool and smooth against my legs, but I found no comfort there. My hands spun and gripped the fabric, *God please make them stop, please.* I listened to the conversation drift down the hall.

"She's my stepdaughter an' she ain't quite right. You know what I mean?" Milda said breathing hard. "You have no idea about this one. I can't control her, she just falls to the floor screaming, in hysterics," Milda lied.

"That may be, ma'am, but I can't leave her here. She says, you beat her and she wants to go home. I'll have to take her into protective custody until we can get this thing sorted out," the officer explained.

A few minutes later, Isla came into the bedroom, still crying. Her face had bright, red blooms that were starting to swell. She grabbed some clothes and threw them into a suitcase and left with the police. She didn't say good-bye. I wouldn't see Isla again for a year when Maggie and I would be taken home too.

My father didn't acknowledge the incident. I would find out later, that the beating, now documented, held valuable leverage for Maggie and our mother, because they had a plan.

My parents didn't have a formal custody arrangement and our father did not support his children financially. Their contentious relationship barred any communication or agreement on what might be best for us. My mother learned from Maggie that letters she had written to me over the past year were intercepted by

Milda. I wouldn't know it for years. I thought my mother didn't love me or want me because she never contacted me.

"Is this all the mail?" I'd ask flipping through the pile on the counter, hoping for a letter from my mother.

"Ain't nothin in there for you. She don't care nothin' about you honey," Milda would say.

Our mother was furious at Isla's beating and wanted Maggie to come home. "It's time to come home Maggie, they've brainwashed Nita so just come on home." "I'm not leaving Nita here. I don't care if I have to stay; I'm not coming back without her."

Milda beat Maggie only once during the time she lived with us. She was more than Milda bargained for—unlike Dickey, me or Isla, Maggie fought back.

The new school year began and it was only weeks after Isla's beating that our father was invited to go frog gigging, something popular with his crowd. The men would hunt giant frogs in the pitch-dark, shining bright lights to blind the frogs long enough to impale them with a three-pronged spear. Their legs would be removed, deep-fried, and consumed as a delicacy.

"I want to go too, Dell. Why can't I go?" Milda's voice was strained and emotional from behind their bedroom door.

"Because. "You're not goin'. It ain't for women, Milda. It'll be cold and muddy, baby. You don't want to go."

She argued further, "Yes I do, Dell. You know I don't care nothin' about the cold or mud."

"Jesus H Christ, Milda, I'll be back in a few days" he said. My father slammed out of the house.

Milda began to drink heavily and pouted like a sullen teenager. "I'm goin' out tonight," she said. "I don't need your daddy to have a good time. No sir, I don't."

She lifted a cigarette to her lips. Her foot bounced nervously as she leaned into the round, lighted, makeup mirror and drew dark, liner around her big eyes.

Maggie fluttered around the kitchen watching her. She had been receiving letters from our mother through the counselors at school, and Milda resented being outsmarted by Dell's ex-wife.

She began taunting, Maggie hurling degrading remarks about our mother. Her speech was slurred, "You know your mother is just a useless bitch, right?" With a nasty smirk, she looked up from the mirror its yellow glow reflecting on her face, creating pinpoints of light in her dark eyes.

Maggie glared at her silently with open disdain.

Milda continued, "In fact, I think she is a pig! Yes, a pig!" she screamed.

She lurched from her chair and moved inches away from, Maggie's face, "Call your mother a pig!" she shrieked. She stabbed her index finger into Maggie's chest forcing her to step backward with each tiny shove. "Right now, I said to call her a pig!"

I sat at the kitchen table, mute with fear. Glancing at Maggie I was struck by her eyes, hard and blue as marbles. She had a soft spray of freckles across her high, cheekbones, framed by curly, chestnut hair. Maggie and I looked remarkably alike, with the exception of our hair color. She had no response to Milda's rant except the tightening of lips, and balling of fists, which hung motionless at her sides.

Milda slapped Maggie across the face with each new verbal assault.

"Call your mother a pig." *Slap*. "Say it!" *Slap*. "Say, My mother's a pig!" *Slap*.

Maggie's back was pressed tightly against the wall. Suddenly, she screamed,

"No, I won't! You're the stinking pig!" Her face was red and, in that moment, Maggie changed. Her hatred was so pure I could feel it in the air, a density that covered her like a shield.

Maggie punched Milda hard in the chest and then shoved her backwards sending her sprawling across the kitchen floor.

Maggie did not stop. She reached over and grabbed a knife from the counter.

Milda cowered on the floor and Maggie warned her, "If you ever come near me again, I will cut your throat! Do you hear me? I will cut you while you sleep!"

Her voice shook with vengeance, and her lips curled in a deep snarl, and her eyes said she meant it.

Silence filled the kitchen. I had never fought back and I was completely stunned at the anger that exploded out of Maggie. With the knife still clutched tightly in her hand, Maggie fled into the night.

Milda pulled herself up and herded me into the pick-up truck to search for my sister. Babbling to herself, she made threats as we drove. "Wait till I get my hands on you, girly. I can't believe I put up with this shit! Juvenile delinquents! Just wait and see what happens, just wait!"

Maggie was smart enough to keep to the ditches at the side of the roads, and while I could guess where she would go, I didn't dare tell. After driving around randomly for a while, Milda headed to Maggie's best friend Teresa's house.

Teresa lived alone with her mother in an old house on a lot of hard, cracked dirt. The only sign of life was a giant tree that grew in the middle of the barren sprawl.

Milda swung the truck under the tree, bouncing over the curb.

She stumbled when she stepped down from the cab and made her way to the front door banging on it violently.

"Well, my God," Teresa's mother said, as she opened the door. "It's kinda late, ain't it? What's wrong?"

She was in her nightgown, her hair ratty and her multiple chins quivering as she spoke. She knew all about Milda—the letters to school, the drinking, the whole story. She knew, too, that Maggie was sitting high above our heads in the tree. It was late and pitch black. Teresa's mom did not turn on the porch light.

Milda never saw Maggie's small form in the headlights of the truck as we pulled in, but I did.

Scared and angry, Maggie sat perched silently on a limb until we left. She stayed at Teresa's house until our father picked her up a few days later.

Like so many events in the past, I never heard my father speak of the beating or its ramifications. It was as if it never happened.

Milda never beat Maggie violently again, although none of us could escape her wild, random swings that left red welts and bruises. I hid my marks in shame, while Maggie showed hers to anyone who would look. She stayed in secret contact with our mother through the counselors at school.

One afternoon, I was unexpectedly summoned to the principal's office. I pulled the heavy office door open and the sounds of voices and ringing phones rushed toward me. The air was laden with a faint scent of fresh ink and school lunches. I laid my blue slip on the counter.

"Oh yes, honey," the secretary said as she pointed down the hall, "you go on down to see Mrs. Fielding, the counselor."

Anxiety overwhelmed me. I was surprised when I entered the room and saw Maggie sitting next to the counselor who sat rigidly perched on the edge of her chair. Her dark hair hung in tight curls on her forehead, softening the harsh rim of the glasses that monopolized her face.

"Come on in and sit down, sweetheart," the stranger said to me.

I am not going to sit down and I am not your sweetheart, I thought bitterly.

Maggie said, "It's okay, she knows."

She knows what? I thought.

I stood in stony silence as another woman entered the small office. She quietly shut the door behind her. She carried an instamatic camera, the kind that spits out a photo as soon as you take it. Sweat coated my palms and my stomach churned.

"It's okay," Maggie said, again. "They just want to take some pictures of the bruises on your back."

Anger and embarrassment flooded through me. I looked at Maggie, *How could you tell?* I could not believe that Maggie would humiliate me this way, in front of people. Embarrassment moved through me like an electrical current and I glared hatefully at my sister who sat with silent, tears, gliding down her face.

The next several moments were a blur. I cried and lifted my shirt, exposing my shame. The camera's flash exploded, and though I heard voices, tears pooled in my ears, drowning out their words.

In truth, Maggie saved us both with the boldness of her actions. She had allowed pictures to be taken of herself all along, showing the results of Milda's blows. Our mother used the pictures as leverage.

She said to our father over the phone, "Dell, you bring them home or I'll call the authorities so fast, you won' t know what hit you."

"And just what do you think you can do, Caroline? These girls are better off with me."

"I have pictures. The counselors at school took them. They are clear evidence of Milda's handy work. You should see them, bruises all over Nita. And let's not forget the little incident with Isla last summer. I have pictures of her too and a documented police report. I'll have that bitch thrown in jail for child abuse. Don't push me, Dell. Bring them home."

Our father was driving trucks after being laid off from his position with the airlines. He loaded us up, and drove us across the country, in a big rig to our mother, who waited with steely determination. She didn't know how she would support us; my father never paid a cent in child support. She couldn't know the dangerous roads that lay ahead.

Maggie had become a warrior and protected me at every turn. Yet that year, at age twelve, she had begun to steal Milda's vodka, hiding a bottle in her locker at school.

It was the beginning of years of struggle with alcohol and drug abuse. She would eventually become sober, but not before a long and tiring fight. Maggie still carries a look in her bright, blue eyes that warns others to tread lightly.

THE BOY - ACCIDENT

When he regained consciousness, bile rose in his throat and his body shook in a violent spasm. Intense pain radiated from his right arm and rendered him unconscious again.

The nurse hurried into the room where the young man lay. She reached for the thick bandages that covered his arm just as his doctor entered.

"How's the patient this morning?" he asked.

"He had a restless night, but he is stable now, doctor. I was just about to change his dressings."

The young nurse loved this doctor, swooned over him really. He was the best surgeon in the state and had saved the young man's arm in a groundbreaking surgery. Any other surgeon would have amputated it. The young man's elbow was now a solid piece of bone and steel rods, fused together with nuts and bolts. He would never be able to bend it again, but, he would have an arm and a hand that, with any luck, would function.

"I want him monitored carefully. We don't want him to become unstable and lose what took a miracle to save."

The surgery would change the practice of amputations, nation-wide, offering surgeons alternatives to the removal of badly damaged limbs. The doctor knew this procedure would change his patient's life-and his own too.

"No, of course not, doctor. We'll watch him."

Months passed while the young man lay in the hospital, desperately trying to heal. He was in significant pain and had no memory of how the accident happened. When his mother visited, she talked non-stop about how "they would pay."

"Don't you worry none. I got a lawyer who's gonna get a settlement and those sonsabitches'll pay." Bernadette promised.

"But nobody did it, Ma. I can't remember what happened, maybe it was my fault."

"Oh now, don't you worry. You just get better so's you can come home. I'll take care of it."

"But what about all the school I'm missin, Ma?"

"Theys probly gonna have to send you to school and pay for that too. Don't worry."

The young man began to pass the time fantasizing about going to school and learning to be an ace mechanic. He loved working on cars and was intuitive about taking them apart and fixing what was wrong. *Maybe I'll open my own service station.* He pictured it all as the nurse administered more painkillers.

Bernadette spent those months fighting and negotiating a settlement from the gas station where her son had worked. The tire machine had malfunctioned, sending a metal rim flying into the air, maiming her boy.

The final settlement would take two years, but eventually a large check was sent to Bernadette for her son. It didn't matter that he was now nineteen, his mother cashed the check and her son boiled with anger when he never got a penny. The anger turned to rage and it took all his strength to hide his disgust with his mother. *She is a conniving and devious woman who needs to be punished.* These thoughts tumbled in the dark recesses of his mind.

5

I fished a quarter from the pocket of my jeans and fingered its warmth before slipping it into the jukebox. I knew what song to play.

He'd played it before, looking in my direction first, but pretending not to. I was considered "jailbait" at thirteen. He was twenty-one.

Aaron was his name. He was lean and had green eyes that were bright against his summer tan and auburn hair. He had a certain charisma that drew me to him.

I watched as he bent over the pool table and easily made his shot. He didn't pause as he moved to another. Two-ball in the corner pocket. Six-ball off the bank to the opposite corner. One-ball in the side. He tipped his cue, pointing to each destination before striking.

His roommate, Dan, rubbed the tiny, blue cube of chalk against the tip of his cue, waiting for a turn he knew wouldn't come. His blond, wavy hair was loose to his shoulders like Jesus. Blue eyes bulged on his face and his energy was wild and unpredictable. He gave me the creeps.

"Hey there, Sugar Drawers." he said, looking at me with a filthy smirk.

"That's enough of that language," Pappy said from behind the grill, his back to Dan.

"Shit. She knows it, Pappy. She brings it in here every day. Prick teasing and flaunting it right under our noses. You think we can't smell it?" Dan said.

"Shut up, Dan. Leave her alone," Aaron said, sinking the black eight ball in the side pocket, finishing their game.

"Mmm, yeah. Okay," Dan said. He laid down his pool stick and acknowledged his loss.

We were in Tuck's, a neighborhood grill that served burgers, hot sandwiches and homemade coleslaw.

Shiny, chrome barstools with bright red seats were fixed beneath a countertop where most people ate. A jukebox and the new Pac-Man game sat near the entrance. Toward the rear, was a pair of pool tables that were always busy. You had to place fifty cents on the table's edge, write your name on the chalkboard affixed to the wall behind them, and wait your turn.

Pappy owned the place with his son, Robert. It was Pappy's fatherly nature that first drew me back, day after day.

From behind the counter Pappy slid a red plastic basket of hot, crispy fries to me with a wink. "Oops," he said. "My mistake. You eat them." Suddenly from outside, a man screaming profanities interrupted the easy mood of the lunch crowd. Everyone looked toward the front window. A man in baggy jeans and a wife-beater t-shirt stood shouting at a young woman.

"What the hell! Who do you think you are? You stupid skank!" He grabbed her arm and jerked her toward him. "I'll knock the snot right out of you, woman!" He raised his arm ready to backhand her. She ducked her head, putting up her forearm in a protective gesture. "No, Ray!"

"You know I'll do it!" he screamed. His energy field looked thick and sluggish, like he was high. The anger moved sharp and tight in the slush.

Aaron gently laid his pool stick on the table and went to the door.

"You don't want to do that here, buddy. Let her go and walk the other way."

"What's it to you?" the man hissed.

Aaron stood silent, the glass door resting against his back. He locked eyes with the stranger. "I mean it, buddy," he said.

The man was bigger than Aaron and angrier, yet he let go of the woman with a shove. She stumbled backwards. He turned away and said, "She ain't worth a nickel anyway."

The woman rubbed her upper arm and looked down. Her mouth was slightly open and revealed a missing front tooth.

"Do you need a ride somewhere?" Aaron asked the distraught woman.

"Yes," she said in voice choked with tears.

"I'll be right back. Lemme get my keys."

In a few strides, Aaron grabbed his keys from a small table and left.

The only sound in the place was the song, "One Of These Nights" by the Eagles, that I'd played on the jukebox only moments before. My heart ached and my stomach churned with want for Aaron. He looked like a hero in my thirteen-year-old eyes. I desperately wanted someone to save me too.

Maggie and I had found Tuck's shortly after we'd returned to our mother's. Without child support, she struggled to make ends meet. She got a new job and we moved to a small two- bedroom condo in a new town. Isla, Maggie and I shared one bedroom. Karina had just graduated from high school and our mother told her it was time she made it on her own. "You can't come Karina. I can't afford it. You'll have to get a job and toughen up." None of us knew the truth. We believed Karina simply moved out.

Maggie and I walked past Tuck's on the way to school every day. For weeks, after school I went there hoping to see Aaron, praying he would notice me. I'd choose tight pants and line my eyes with thick, dark liner that I hoped made me look older. I searched for ways to draw his attention. Then it came to me. *Learn to play pool.*

I took a billiards course offered as an elective during my freshman year of high school. I became very good winning tournaments that gained me trophies and custom pool sticks. I practiced as often as I could at Tuck's to impress Aaron. I thought about him constantly, doodling his name surrounded by hearts, rainbows, happy faces and the word "love" on notebooks during class.

Aaron played pool with me one afternoon and admired my growing skills. "You're pretty good. You must be practicing." My insides squirmed when he looked at me. I wanted to squeal with pride at his compliment. *Yes, yes! I am good! Do you like me now? It doesn't matter how old I am. I love you!* I wanted to show him that we were meant to be together. But, he kept his distance.

Frustrated, I showed up at his house one Saturday morning with a broom and dustpan.

"I'm here to clean the house for you guys," I said to a bleary- eyed Dan, who stood in boxer shorts, rubbing his face.

"What for?"

"So you can have a clean house. I'll do it for free." "Whatever. I'm going back to bed." Dan said, shuffling down the hall.

I showed up on weekends and after school. I desperately wanted Aaron to notice just what I would do for him. When he showered, I snuck into his room breathing in his smell. I finally felt close to him. I felt I had a chance to make him love me.

"Nita!" Aaron called from his room one morning, shortly after I'd arrived.

I scurried down the hall trying to control the silly smile that stretched across my face. "What do you need Aaron?"

Aaron lifted the cover on his bed and said, "I need you to come keep me warm."

My heart bloomed as I moved toward his bed. *Oh my god! He does love me!* I was delirious with happiness.

Out of bed he treated me as if nothing had happened between us. I believed it was because he didn't trust me and that over time I could change his mind. It was rumored that he'd been hurt badly by his ex-girlfriend. They'd had a child together, but the relationship was over. She stopped by one Saturday afternoon with a sweet blond-haired boy who I assumed was their son. I was struck by her beauty and envious of their relationship.

"Is Aaron here?" she asked, eyeing me warily and gripping her child's hand.

My heart was pounding as I replied, "I think he's in his room." I'd just left his bed moments before and I felt like I'd been caught doing something I shouldn't.

They sat together outside in the backyard watching the child play. I heard snippets of conversation float in on the breeze.

"Hey, little man, come show Daddy what you got." Aaron reached for the boy who toddled toward him. Happiness glowed on the child's face. He extended his little arm making an offering to his father. "Che, chk." came the garbled reply. Aaron lifted the boy into his lap kissing him repeatedly on his face while the child squirmed and giggled with delight.

My heart clenched. *What a beautiful child*, I thought. *She's beautiful too. I'll never have a chance.* I watched through the kitchen window as the bright afternoon sun and spring breeze painted a perfect picture of a small family. I would never see the woman or child again, nor would Aaron. She refused all contact and for years I thought her cruel and condemned for keeping Aaron from his son.

I was surprised when Aaron had invited me into his bed and I'd felt so hopeful. For me, his invitation meant he loved me. Having sex with me proved it. That's what sex was, right? An expression of love. At least that's what I thought.

Two weeks later, on a Sunday afternoon, I swept a pile of dirt from their kitchen floor. *Where does all this crap come from?* I wondered. I'd already filled the sink with soap and water, dipping in the long, ropey tendrils of the mop that reminded me of my child-hood. As a child, the mop was a beautiful princess who lived in a garden that was my backyard. I'd play for hours holding the mop, watching the strands of cloth swing, and pretending it was long, golden hair. Together we would dance with the prince at imaginary balls.

Aaron, Dan, and four other male friends sat drinking and

smoking pot in the spare bedroom of their house. It wasn't unusual. There was a constant flow of young guys that came and went.

Dan called from the room. "Hey, Sugar Drawers! Come in here a minute." Something in his voice made me nervous. I hated Dan. I gripped the molding around the door and stuck my head in the room. Empty beer bottles, overflowing ashtrays, and an empty pint of rum and Jack Daniels lay scattered on the floor. Smoke was heavy in the air.

"What?" I asked nervously.

The energy in the room felt dangerous. It was thick with testosterone, although I couldn't name it. My body buzzed with alarm.

Dan said, "We want to talk to you. Don't be scared, come in here."

Dan straddled a wooden chair turned backwards. A baseball cap was pulled low to his brow, his long hair tied back at his neck.

I stepped forward and jerked with a start at the sound of the door slamming behind me. The men sat in a circle around me. My heart pumped. I squeezed the dustpan handle and fixed my eyes on the floor. Fear stiffened my limbs. I waited.

Dan started the talking. "Tell me why we shouldn't take turns with you right now? We know that's what you come here for."

I couldn't speak or swallow. His crude words stung me. A distant ringing began to sound in my ears. I kept my head down. Humiliation uncoiled itself and raced through my body. *You deserve this,* it whispered.

"We've decided that's exactly what we're gonna do, Sugar Drawers. Today. Right now."

My body absorbed a jumble of thoughts and feelings all at once. I heard the random thoughts of the men in the room. *Shit, she's really scared. Is Dan really gonna do it?*

He's crazy. Look at her ass though, m-m-m-m.

I couldn't tell who thought what but I felt their mixed intention slice through me. I *knew* if something sexual started, it would be like a feeding frenzy. There would be no stopping it. I felt like I was surrounded by a pack of wild dogs.

Terrified, my mind jumped. *I just come to be with Aaron. Aaron, why are you doing this? Please, don't hurt me. Aaron, please. I know you love me. Why are you doing this?* My skin felt like stinging nettles and I was confused. Aaron sat silently among the men; it was a dagger in my soul. The energy in the room swallowed me, suffocated me. *Oh God, what should I do?*

I lost track of time. I could no longer hear their words. Bile, slick and wet shot from the back of my throat filling my mouth. I swallowed forcing it down. I couldn't believe Aaron would be part of this. The agony of that truth pulsed like a fever under my skin.

Suddenly, Dan stood up and moved toward me.

I'm going to vomit.

"That's enough." Aaron said. "Open the door and let her out." No one moved or spoke.

"Open the door!" Aaron screamed, standing up.

"Next time, you won't be so lucky." Dan promised.

I bolted on wooden legs. Tears blurred my vision. I ran from the house. After several blocks I collapsed in hysterics. My body shook with fear and the realization of what had almost happened. *I am so stupid. Stupid, stupid, stupid.* Confusion clouded my mind. *Why did this happen? Does it mean Aaron doesn't love me? Why did he make them let me go?*

I sat tucked beside a hedge and cement steps on a stranger's front lawn. Pain in my gut clutched hard, bending me over. I opened my mouth and surrendered to my sickness.

"Ohhh-ohhh- God," I roared tipping my head toward the sky. "Why, why? What is wrong with me? Why does everyone hate me?" I cried until I ran out of tears. My body ached as the fantasy of being loved crumbled. I wanted to be numb. I wanted to disappear. I wanted to die.

I didn't go back to Aaron's house nor would I see him for months.

The pot I'd recently begun smoking was no longer enough to escape my pain and I started dangerously devouring drugs. Weeks after the crushing episode at Aaron's, I had my first overdose.

My body lay lifeless, face down in the grass like a corpse. Drool flowed freely as I struggled to draw breath. Efforts to turn my head and close my mouth to the dirt and grit that filled it were in vain. I managed to move my jaw up and down like a cow gnawing at the earth. A low ringing filled my ears and while I knew where I was, I realized I might die undetected by the mothers and children playing near me on the swing sets and slides of the park. I felt a presence hover over me like a reverse shadow, but I was unable to communicate with it. It reminded me of Maggie's angel and I held onto the memory for as long as I was conscious.

Several hours had passed by the time Maggie found me. I had snorted a deadly mixture of PCP and cocaine. When I opened my eyes I was lying on a bed in an unfamiliar room. The curtains billowed inward from the breeze. Maggie held my ankle tightly and forced my knee to bend gliding my foot toward my chest and out again while she cradled a phone receiver tucked firmly between her ear and shoulder.

"Yes," she said. "I am doing that. Mm'hm, I don't know how much she did. Yes, it was definitely PCP mixed with coke."

She listened intently to the person on the other end. Fearful I would die she'd called the Drug Hotline and was speaking with a nurse. She glanced up and looked directly at me. "She just opened her eyes," she said, exhaling her pent-up anxiety. After another moment she said, "Okay, I will. Thank you."

She hung up the phone and pulled me out of bed forcing my body upright and walked with me back and forth; tiny bits of grit still crunched between my teeth. I felt boneless, a replica of Gumby dancing a ballet.

"Jesus Christ," Maggie snarled. "You're a complete idiot. You scared the shit out of me."

We were across the parking lot in another condo in our complex and through the open window we heard a car' s engine and Maggie looked out.

"That's just great. Mom's home." And as the car door slammed, she said, "Come on, Nita, Knock it off. You better get a grip."

It took a couple of hours of forced repetitive movement before I began to feel normal, but thanks to Maggie's intervention I recovered.

Much of this period is hazy, but in spite of the drugs the voice in my mind and the *light-body* remained constant and clear.

The *light-body,* would appear without warning, sometimes multiple times a day. It wasn't as big as a person - more the size of a large dog- and had no real body shape. *It's like a weird reflection*, I thought. It looked like heat waves with a hazy glow.

When I saw it hovering, I'd glance around the room to confirm I alone saw the energy. From my best recollection, the *light-body* appeared on a regular basis only after my traumatic incident at Aaron's house.

Days after my overdose, out of the blue our mother said, "You girls aren't going to school tomorrow. We each have appointments with a psychic named Boots. We'll spend the day together and have lunch."

We all knew that this was an extravagant expense and completely out of the ordinary. We rarely had family outings, money was simply too tight. We skipped Christmas two years in a row because we couldn't afford it, so this was really a surprise. Our mother had become increasingly interested in "psychic phenomena." I was unclear as to what the term actually meant and I didn't share my unique experiences with her. I had no clue what they were or that I might be psychic. Despite the cost, we each had a private reading—a half-hour that I will never forget.

Boots sat Indian style on a giant beanbag chair. Her office reeked of incense. Scattered on the floor across from her were several bean-bags in various colors and sizes. I nervously sat in one and stared at the woman.

Her belly protruded like a Buddha, and her face cascaded into her neck as though she had no chin. Her brown eyes glistened. "Welcome. Come closer and let me see you and hold your hands."

I did as I was told, staying as silent as a monk.

Inhaling deeply, she smiled and said, "Oh yes, you are a mystic, a seer. You will help many people in your life. You are gifted. You've suffered a great deal of pain and I' m afraid you have a rocky road ahead of you."

Her insight surprised me. *How does she know if I've suffered? What does she see?* I *knew* she was right that I would help people, I'd always *known* it, but like much of the *knowing,* I couldn't fully grasp it. My self-esteem was so low that I couldn't imagine doing anything good. Still, I hung on her every word. I desperately wanted her to be right. I leaned forward and blurted, "I had an abortion. I killed a soul." Tears welled and I couldn't believe I'd told her of my sin.

I had suspected I was pregnant days after the disastrous incident at Aaron's and I was terrified to tell my mother. I gathered all of my courage and approached her one morning while she was getting ready for work.

"Mom, I think I'm pregnant," I confessed.

"Oohh, Nita. Jesus Christ." My mother's body sagged and then went rigid. "I'll make an appointment with my gynecologist, and we will take care of it."

That was the end of any discussion. I worried that the *light- body* and God would be angry, but I was relieved that my mother would help without condemning me. I'd had the abortion only days before our session with Boots.

Boots sat in silence for a moment. Then she gently squeezed my hands and said, "You are not powerful enough to kill a soul. None of us are. Before we incarnate on this earth plane, we choose our parents, siblings, sex, social economic situation, and more because these things best support our life path and what we plan to learn. There are no mistakes. The soul that moved through your body knew you would not keep it. It was the soul's choice. You helped each other, and we cannot know the how's or whys on this level of consciousness. They don't matter. To know them changes nothing."

"But I killed it," I squeaked, openly crying.

"I know that's what some would have you believe. Souls don't die, human bodies do. A soul has many choices. Sometimes the soul wants to lower its vibration and prepare for incarnation. They may use your body to do so, moving in and out of a physical form. It's an agreement that was made before you were born and many will share in the lesson of your experience. The doctor, nurses, you, your family, or those touched in some way by your action will have their own lesson. Again, we don't know. Have you heard of SIDS disease?"

"You mean when babies die in their sleep for no reason?"

"Yes. As long as the soft spot in the crown is open, a soul is free to come and go. Sometimes the soul has either previously agreed to leave, or they make the choice to leave and try again. We are reflections of God and we have free will. There are very few accidents although they do occur. In your case, it' s doubtful. You agreed to assist a soul and the soul assisted you, there is no blame."

My body shimmied with goose bumps and I felt the truth in her words. Encouraged I went on. "I see stuff sometimes," I said. She didn't ask what I saw but said, "Of course you do, It'll be alright. Do you know how to meditate?"

"No." I said. She said 'of course you do' like it was perfectly normal. I thought.

Boots said, "Meditation is the highway to enlightenment. You should meditate every day to ground your energy and open up to your inner guidance. It will help you."

Boots instructed me to bring in light through the crown of my head, letting it flow down one arm, out of my palm, and into the other creating a circle of light. I found comfort in the practice, and would meditate sporadically throughout my youth. While nothing in my behavior changed at the time, I tucked away the information and would use it later in life. I'd eventually learn countless other methods of meditation until I made it and prayer part of my daily life.

I wanted to believe Boots. I wanted to be special. I liked the idea of being a "mystic." Although I didn't understand what the word meant, it felt good when she said it. Unfortunately, I wasn't ready to embrace everything that she told me. I simply couldn't believe I harbored anything good or special.

On the drive home Maggie chirped, "That was really cool. Boots told me that I will have three kids and, she said I will never be rich, but I won't have to worry about money, either. Cool, huh?" And then Isla said, "She said I was an opera singer in a past life." We all laughed because Isla was tone deaf and couldn't sing at all.

"I guess that's why you can't carry a tune now, huh?" Maggie teased.

My mother said, "We talked about my past lives, and I remember one where I was an Indian and had such a happy life. Not like this terrible one. She said I don't have to come back and reincarnate if I don't want to and I'm not. After this life, I am done."

What pure bullshit, I thought. I didn't believe what Boots said about past lives. *Anyone could say that kind of crap.* I kept my thoughts to myself and said, "She said that I am a mystic, a seer. She said I will use my gift in this life to help people, and she showed me how to meditate." *Let's see what they think of that.*

Silence rang in the car and I assumed nobody believed me. *Maybe it sounds like such bullshit they think it's a lie,* I reasoned. I had been dubbed the "flakey" child early on in life. My mother would look at me and say, "Jesus, Nita, you're such a flake, you live in your own world."

And I did, not because I was unmoored or stupid. The Clairs often kept me absorbed and distracted, but no one would know about them until years later. Maggie's predictions would come true, as would mine. I didn't tell my family about the *light-bodies* or voices. I worried I was crazy and I suspected no one would believe me anyway. I didn't believe it myself. It seemed to be just like the past lives statement, impossible to prove. Still, I felt hopeful after our time with Boots, though I wasn't sure why. I held onto her words, burying them in my subconscious.

Maggie and I sold drugs in order to get ours for free. A new type of pot was on the scene called Thai-Stick. Touted to be better than anything available, it was in high demand with potheads. We were told only one person had it- a family man who was the friend of an older couple Maggie knew.

The man's name was Roger. He lived in an affluent part of town where large homes sat in neat rows and climbed steep hills. We parked our old crappy car in front of his tidy house and rang the bell. We were greeted with the smell of pot-roast. Fleetwood Mac's "You Can Go Your Own Way" rang from strategically-placed speakers, making the carpeted floor beneath us pound with the music's beat. The matching furniture looked unused and perfectly placed.

Roger stood with his feet apart in the middle of the room. He clasped his hands behind his back and rocked on the balls of his feet. His head was bald, yet thick, black, curly hair covered his exposed arms and legs. His face was broad with a permanent smile that showed perfect teeth.

"What can I do you for?" he asked through his creepy leer. "Whatever you need, I got it, no problemo there."

He reminded me of a giant cartoon wolf who licked his hungry snout as he spoke through smoke and mirrors. The air tightened around me and the voice said, *"He touches his girls. He has sexual intent. See the sadness down the hallway."* I turned my head and peered down the hallway adorned with photos of his family. A large colored image of a young girl missing her two front teeth smiled at me. Goose flesh raced over my skin and I *knew.* I saw in my mind's eye the stolen moments in the dark and I felt the fear and dread that hung there. Rogers's deep voice brought me back to where I stood.

"We're havin' a little part-e-e tonight, if you care to indulge. A little skipidy-do-dah to celebrate the wife's birthday. It'll be a good time, if ya know what I mean," he said, raising his eyebrows and smiling like the Cheshire cat.

"I'm gonna wait in the car," I said and hurried out the door. I felt like I'd been doused in his sickness and wanted to wipe myself clean. I looked back and watched Rogers's body energy recede as he spun his tales of a happy home. In this instance, I believed what I *knew,* I listened to the voice and got out as quickly as I could.

That same year I was introduced to a man more than twice my age. His name was Angel. He, too, was a friend of Roger's and the older couple that Maggie knew.

Angel was thirty-five and I was fifteen. He showered me with attention. He told me I was beautiful and special. After the traumatic and confusing episode at Aaron's, Angel's flattery was like a delicacy I desperately craved.

He had coffee-colored skin and a quiet demeanor. He took me

down a road of utter self- destruction, the likes of which I hadn't encountered. My mother knew about our relationship yet never intervened or restricted me from seeing him. I assumed that she felt he might be a good influence because of his age.

One afternoon, as Angel and I sat in the bedroom of his condo talking, he casually placed a bundle between us on the bed. Inside was a two - inch wide rubber band tourniquet- the kind used when drawing blood- as well as a syringe, needle, spoon, eyedropper and small piece of cotton. I watched as he mixed cocaine and speed in the spoon dropping dollops of water to dissolve his tincture. He then dipped the cotton onto the spoon and filled the syringe. Holding the apparatus upright he flicked his middle finger against it to force any air bubbles, wrapped his bicep tightly with the tourniquet, and gently inserted the needle. A drop of velvety red blood, danced in the liquid and he released the contents into his arm. His eyes fluttered closed.

I was fascinated. I laid my arm across his lap and said, "I want to try."

"No way," he replied. "This is not for you."

"Why not? You do it. What's the big deal?" I countered. He looked at me and neither of us spoke for a moment.

"I've been doing this for a long time and I don't want to be the one who gets you involved."

"Why not, Angel? Do you regret it?" I asked accusingly.

"No, but I can handle it."

"Oh, and I can't? I'm the little girl, is that right?" I sniped.

"Ahhhh," Angel sighed. "I didn't mean that. Okay, I know you can make your own decisions. If you want to, I'll help you."

And he "fixed" me with his syringed demon. My stomach was hollow. I knew this was taboo and my ears rang with sirens of warning. My pulse raced as the drugs flowed through my veins and I wondered if my heart would explode. Even before the syringe was empty I could not escape the whisper from the voice in my head, *Is this you really want? You begin down a path you may not wish to take. Listen to your inner voice,* it said. And when I looked up, there in the corner hovering like a cloud was the *light- body*. Incredibly, I felt no judgment from the presence, only a comforting love.

I *knew* from the beginning I could not continue this way. For the first time I feared ignoring the voice. The truth was I didn't feel anything special for Angel. I didn't like having sex with him, I didn't find him interesting, and I had no real attraction or affection toward him. He was kind to me, and supplied me with free drugs and helped me escape the negative environment that was home. That was it. It was a tradeoff and nothing more.

I *knew* I had a window of time before my choices would bring consequences I could not bear. I told no one I was using a needle for my high, especially not Maggie. I could hear her voice ringing in my ears. *Are you a complete idiot? Don't you know better than this?*

For much of my teenage life I lived peripherally, not fully connected with my experiences or choices. I had sex with partners I didn't like or barely knew, and engaged in behavior day after day that brought me no joy. I limited using a needle for my high, afraid of the repercussions that the voice warned me of. When I stopped using intravenous drugs, it was a direct result of heeding my own inner voice and the *knowing*.

The final event was ordinary, no different than the ones that came before, except for the *knowing* that it carried. Angel had reverently unfolded the leather satchel that held the necessary tools. Veins bulged in the soft white valley of my forearm, as the tourniquet hugged my bicep tightly. I pumped my fist. He'd already mixed the cocaine and speed and filled the syringe. He gently pushed the needle into a large awaiting vein. I felt a pinch and watched as it silently disappeared into my flesh. As my heart began its race, I saw a *picture* in my mind's eye of a room that smelled of decay and human feces. A gold couch so filthy it was almost brown was pushed against a wall, its stuffing spilling out through tears like a bleeding wound. Several people were sprawled on the couch or the floor in various states of intoxication. I *knew* they had no homes, and the need to be high was like a putrid film covering their skin. A jumble of frenetic energy filled the room. Silent molecules of death screamed. My stomach clenched with fear and my body tingled with the certainty that this is where I would go if I continued down this path.

I understood that the vision was a warning, and I took what the *knowing* told me seriously. I didn't know if the *pictures* showed me a life that lay ahead, or if I viewed the life of others who were trapped in a drug-induced capsule. Either way I didn't want that life.

In that same instant, I saw Angel in a new way. He repulsed me and I repulsed myself. There was no dramatic break-up. I simply stayed at home more, stopping contact with him, and for a while, with the needle.

THE BOY BECOMES A MAN

The man abandoned any sentiment of boyhood ideals or notions of fairness and integrity. Instead, he crawled on the ground, a predator in the dark. He smiled as he recalled his warning to his girlfriend, "You better be careful in the dark. You never know who's out there."

It was his way of telling her who she was dealing with, but the stupid bitch didn't get it. He moved, flat against the dirt, immune to the sharp rocks and shards of glass. He imagined himself a snake, sleek and stealthy. He no longer feared the dark as he had as a child; rather he embraced it as the giver of transformation. He'd discovered that he could be anything in the dark.

He reached for his binoculars and watched the woman through the window. The light was bright inside giving expression to her every move. He knew her. He had feelings for her. But women were dogs and couldn't be trusted—this one was no exception. As he watched, he felt his excitement rise and harden against the earth.

His mind wandered back to a couple of weeks before. He'd been watching another dog and surprised her by sneaking quietly through an unlocked screen door late at night. He had been ready with his mask and gun but the woman's boyfriend, lying half asleep on their bed, had surprised him. The man hadn't seen him. *The prick did not have his car parked in front.*

"I'll kill her, you dumbass," he warned when the boyfriend tried to stand up. "Put the pillowcase over your head and leave your arms at your side. Lie face down." The woman was as silent as a corpse when he pointed the gun at her and said, "Take your clothes off and hurry up."

When she was naked and shivering with fear, he couldn't get hard, no matter what he did. Things hadn't gone as planned. The boyfriend wouldn't shut up, "Hey man, you don't have to do this. Just leave and we won't tell. Seriously, man, please."

"Shut up! Shut the hell up," he'd yelled.

He'd panicked and realized he had to get out of there. He snatched a handful of the woman's hair smelling its flowery fragrance and forced her on the bed. "Stay face down and don't move for a half hour or I will come back and kill you both."

The boyfriend finally found his balls and chased after him. He'd swung a bat that narrowly missed his head but connected with his arm, breaking it. The man had to go to a doctor that night to get a splint. He made up a story for his friends that he'd whipped some ass at the local 7- eleven. Everyone knew what punks hung out there.

The boyfriend had ruined everything. It was disappointing and embarrassing, but he wouldn't make that mistake again. He turned his focus back to the woman in the window.

~

The young woman hummed as she dried her dishes and moved toward the wall where her telephone was mounted.

"Hello?" she said happily. "Oh hi, Honey. (Honey was a girlfriend).

Yes, I would love to go to the fair. That sounds fun. What time did you want to

go?" She shifted her weight to the other foot. "Six would be perfect. What's that? No-no, he has to work, it'll just be me."

The woman massaged her pregnant belly as she hung up the

phone. Suddenly the hairs on the back of her neck rose on a wave of goose bumps. She spun around wildly, her heart racing, certain someone was behind her.

"Oh, my, god," she breathed as her hands shook and she gulped in air. "Oh, my, god, I felt someone breathe on my neck," she whispered to an empty room as she stood shaking in front of her window.

6

I fell backward and my mind spun like a top. The soft fabric of the beanbag chair embraced me and across the room, I saw the *light-body*, hovering again, its energy calm and peaceful. I closed my eyes and when the boy's hands awkwardly caressed my body, I left it. That was how my life went. I got high, cut school, avoided home and engaged in one dangerous activity after the next. Most days I felt like a ghost standing in my own dead shadow.

My eyes looked bloodshot and ragged in the mirrored glass where I quickly snorted my line of "Crank." It seared its way through my nasal passages which were raw pulp. I gagged as it hit my throat leaving the horrid taste of a bitter chemical. *Snorting Draino could not be worse than this shit*, I thought. I needed the speed though to counteract the Quaalude I'd taken earlier. Downers weren't really my thing, but they were free.

The outline of my butt was displayed perfectly in a tight pair of hip-hugger pants, my smooth, flat belly exposed by a midriff top. Behind me a stranger massaged my butt, taking his liberties. *What a dick*, I thought. I was sharing a beanbag chair with him. I didn't know his name. I didn't care. Thick marijuana smoke hung in the air and Peter Frampton blasted from the stereo's speakers. *Shadows grow so long before my eyes, and they're moving across the page. Sudd-en-ly the day turns into night, far away, from the city....ooh baby I love your way.*

I was barely there.

Acid became my drug of choice, although LSD made my already growing psychic abilities more apparent instead of less- something I didn't view as a positive. After dropping acid one night, Maggie and I went home to ride out our high. Our mother was getting ready for bed. She had no idea we were high as we flopped on the couch and waited for "Saturday Night Live" to come on.

As my mother trudged upstairs, I was overcome by her immense sadness. I saw the sadness around her, as thick as syrup. It cut through my high, boring its way into my soul. I *knew* the sadness I felt was not a result of the acid. The *knowing* was present and I recognized it. Her sorrow weighed heavily in my heart and I *knew* it was both old and new. The old sadness had emptiness, an aloneness I could almost hear. There were so many pieces to it like giant roots had snaked from the gloom into her body. It scared the crap out of me.

The *light-body* hovered in the dining room nearby and I could no longer ignore its presence. In the past, closing my eyes could make the image disappear. Now, I would see the energy in my mind's eye and I couldn't shake it, high or not. Wherever I went, it would hover and watch me. My inner voice grew bolder.

Are you waiting? What are you waiting for? It would question. Are you living your destiny?

Oh, my, god, I thought, *I'm so full of it.* But my doubts didn't silence the voice, and a few weeks later it had more to say.

We'd cut school to go sledding in the snow with Maggie's new boyfriend, Robbie. Peter and Allen, friends of Robbie's, went with us. We dropped acid and headed for a hill. Robbie drove his old beat-up station wagon that smelled strongly of pizza and cat piss. Laughing we passed around a joint and a "bota bag" filled with cheap wine.

"Check out the colors in the snow, man. It's cool, like Picasso threw up, man," Alan said as snow-covered hillsides sped by.

Maggie held a book of matches in her hand and, giggling, she said, "Listen to this." She read from the matchbook cover, "Shape up or ship out." Uncontrollable and hysterical laughter followed. I laughed so hard, my stomach and face cramped. I pulled my knees into my chest, gasping for breath. Everyone howled when Alan released a loud, long, fart. We were a pack of wild hyenas, out of control.

The area we chose had large jutting rocks and scattered trees, making sledding dangerous. Snow was an unnatural event in our area. In fact, none of us had ever even seen it there.

I was standing with Maggie and Peter near the top of the ridge, preparing to slide down. Robbie and Allen had already gone and were somewhere below us. Suddenly, Robbie let out a murderous scream. The pain in his voice echoed off the hard surfaces of the mountain. We scrambled down the hillside toward our friends. When we found, Robbie his right leg was twisted at odd angles and he gripped his thigh with both hands, crying in pain. Allen lay on his side in the snow nearby trying to right himself.

"Oh my god! Oh my god, it hurts." Robbie's breath formed clouds of panic in the air. His leg was sickening to look at.

"What are we gonna do, man?" came the frightened response from Allen, who now stood wide-eyed clenching his fists as though breaking invisible rocks.

We stood immobile, paralyzed with fear. I experienced a flash in my mind's eye and saw *pictures* of what'd happened seconds before the accident. I saw Allen, drunk and unstable laughing like the Mad Hatter and flailing his arms awkwardly. He fell sideways off the back of the speeding sled, causing Robbie to turn slightly, careening him into a tree. The disturbing "crack" echoed in my mind.

I felt a collective panic circle the group when I heard the gentle voice in my mind, *Don't worry*, it said. *He will be alright, help is on the way.* I felt the *light-body* hovering although I never saw it.

Relief poured through me because I *knew* Robbie would be okay, but I said nothing. We all pitched in and managed to make it to the top of the ridge carrying him as he screamed out. Allen babbled the entire way, "Holy crap man, this is so screwed up. Shit, what are we gonna do? Fucking-A man, this is bad."

No one else spoke. We found the car and just as we were about to load Robbie, another vehicle approached at a crawl. The driver was an old man, his wife next to him. They craned their necks to see what we were doing and pulled over to help. They knew the area and took Robbie to a hospital. He was immediately given emergency surgery for a broken femur.

For the first time, I was grateful for my message but frightened as well. *Where was this voice coming from, and how does it know things?* I wondered. Suddenly, the voice I'd heard within took on a new meaning. *I have to stop dropping acid*, I thought. I hoped it would quiet the voice and stop me from seeing the *light-body* too, but it didn't.

Weeks after our snow day, as I walked home from school, Aaron drove by. I hadn't seen him in months. Although I'd been deeply hurt, I'd never stopped thinking about him and still wrote his name on my spiraled notebooks, pretending he loved me. He slowed and pulled to the curb.

"You want a ride?" he asked.

He leaned casually out the window, smiling at me. He wore mirrored sunglasses and my heart skipped a beat when I saw him. My stomach filled with the flutter of love and in an instant, I was awash with new hope.

Maggie knew about my close call at Aaron's. She especially hated Dan, but she wasn't a fan of Aaron either. In my mind, I heard her say, "He is such a scumbag," she'd say or "What a loser. What, can you possibly see in him?" She continually warned me to stay away.

Still, I was ecstatic that he stopped for me. "A ride would be great," I said happily. I climbed into his car without hesitation. We pulled away from the curb tires screeching. A thrill ran through me.

"You feel like going for a ride before I drop you off?" Aaron asked.

"Sure," I said, bright with enthusiasm.

We drove with the windows down and music blaring, breathing in nature's fragrant spring air. We passed a tanker truck at high speed on a two-lane road. I saw our image mirrored in the tanker's side as we passed—an image that will be seared forever into my memory.

Maggie got a job as an assistant manager for a fast food restaurant in order to help our mother pay the bills. We'd both curtailed our drug use. Maggie took school more seriously while I took Aaron more seriously. We began to grow apart.

I spent more time at Aaron's, sneaking out at night and returning before school the next morning. I'd carefully fit my fingers inside the cool metal casing of the window and silently pull it back. Cold night air would rush through the small opening of our bedroom where my sisters pretended to be asleep. I' d swing out one leg and then the other through and shimmy onto the condo's rooftop, quietly moving across the sand papery tiles to the fence below. The neighborhoods slept as I hurried along the quiet streets and made my way to Aaron's. I spent four nights a week with him. It became a bone of contention between Maggie and me.

"You better stop sneaking out, Nita," Maggie whispered as I slipped through the window one morning. "Mom knows what you're doing, you stupid ass. She hates him too. You know he can go to jail for statutory rape, right? You better knock it off. I'm not going to protect you when she has his scummy ass locked up."

"Fuck off," I replied.

After school that day I sat on my trundle bed and folded sheets I'd taken from our linen closet to give to Aaron. It wasn't the first batch of goods I'd stolen for him. I'd pilfer through our meager pantry sneaking canned goods, minute rice, and anything else he could eat.

I heard my mother behind me in the hallway. I turned toward my bedroom door surprised she was home. My mother struggled for years with herniated discs. That day, the pain in her back had been too severe for her to go to work. To ease her discomfort, she'd get high on wine and painkillers. I saw that her eyes were wet and unfocused, threaded with red veins creating an odd shine. Her energy was flat.

She leaned against the doorframe looking in at me. a pistol casually dangled from her right hand. I recognized the gun as one she regularly carried in her purse. I looked away, frozen in fear that spread over me like a fever, stinging my skin.

"I drove to that scumbag's house, where you spent the night last night. I was going to knock on the door and blow his head off when he answered, but then I realized that you would never forgive me. You would blame me and hate me for the rest of your life, and then you would just go find yourself another scumbag. So, I decided I would have to kill you instead. I can't stand who you are, and I can't believe you steal from me, for that worthless piece-of-shit, you call a man. You make me sick. I'm just going to kill you and put us both out of our misery."

Her words pierced my heart. I felt my emotions bleed. I was stunned. My mother was rarely home and while we weren't close, I never suspected how she felt. I never imagined that she would want to kill me. I sat fearful and empty as she raised her arm and pointed her gun directly at my head. I heard a harsh click as she pulled back the hammer.

Oh God, I thought squeezing my eyes shut, *she's going to do it.* And I was absolutely immobile, unable to complete a thought. Regret for who I was, fused my throat closed, preventing me from swallowing. A blanket of energy encircled my body but I was pretty sure it couldn't stop a bullet. And then I *knew* she wouldn't do it. Suddenly, the phone rang. The bell was shrill and relentless and screamed endlessly. I felt my heart pounding in my temples.

"Looks like you've been saved by the bell," my mother smirked.

I would learn days later that it was Isla calling from Cadet School, which she'd started a month before. Isla never broke the rules, took drugs or cut school. She was too afraid. She lived for our mother's approval, but she never received it. "I can' t believe I have a child who is so stupid!" our mother would shout at Isla, who'd just stare back with eyes full of pain.

My mother lowered the gun and went to answer the phone. My body shook and my bowels turned to liquid. I ran to the bathroom and locked the door. When I heard her leave, I fled.

I waited in the park for Maggie to finish work and I told her what had happened. I'd expected her to take my side, but Maggie was ambivalent. She hated that I was involved with Aaron and blamed me for upsetting our mother. Maggie had the guns removed from our house, but after that incident my days living at home were numbered. I was fifteen.

As my relationship with Aaron grew, my relationship with Maggie crumbled, and my mother checked out emotionally in a way she never had before. There was a constant storm in our house.

Maggie warned me again to stay away from Aaron. "He is such a lowlife, Nita. He has nothing to offer. What the hell do you see in him?"

"I love him and he is not a, lowlife. You just don' t know him."

"Oh please. I know him and all his scummy, friends." Maggie countered, "He is a piece of crap and you know it. He doesn't love you. Open your eyes. You better get a grip or you won't like what comes next," she threatened.

"What? You're my mother now? You're going to get all high and mighty? I have to do what you say? Go to hell," I screamed and I ran out the door.

I was determined to prove everyone wrong about Aaron. *They don't know him*, I told myself. I refused to see his mean edge as something bad. I stubbornly denied what I *knew* from the beginning- that he was dangerous. When his anger exploded in a jealous rage, I just thought it meant he loved me. I ignored Maggie's warnings until she made good on her threat.

I'd arrived early at my part-time job as a gas station attendant after school. I pushed through the glass door and warm air hit my face blowing my hair back in a welcoming huff. My eyes immediately fell on two tall boxes pushed to the corner of the tiny room. "NITA" was scrawled in black marker across the front of each. Tony greeted me with a quick nod and returned to his task. He mumbled, "Someone dropped those off earlier. Said they were for you."

"Really? I wonder what they are." I moved toward the boxes.

"Girl that left them was kind of a bitch," he offered. "What'd she look like?"

"I don't know. Kinda curly, brown hair." She dropped the boxes outside and yelled, 'These are Nita's 'and then drove off. Bitchy, if you ask me."

It was Maggie, I thought.

I dug through the boxes and my heart sank as the truth settled in.

"Holy crap," I muttered. They're kicking me out. I can't believe it. What am I gonna do?"

"Bummer, man. That sucks. Wish I could help you, man, but you know how it is, the old lady would *not* understand."

"That's cool. I'll find somewhere to go." But my mind was reeling. *Who could I call and what was I going to do?*

I called a school friend, Deanna, who lived nearby. She and her boyfriend picked me up after work. I'd known Deanna since eighth grade and although we ran with different crowds, we were still friends. She had a boyfriend who liked to talk on CB radios and "mud run" in his Jeep. I went home with Deanna that night with no plan or idea where I might go. I was deeply hurt and in a complete state of shock. I sat opposite of Deanna's mom on the coffee table's edge. She held my hands in hers as she spoke.

"Call me mom, everybody does, and tell me what happened." Her eyes held such compassion that I had to look away.

"I don't know," I replied as I shrugged in disbelief. "I got to work after school and all my stuff was there. I guess they don't want me anymore." Tears rimmed my eyes and my body was rigid with rejection.

"OK, doll," she said as she patted my hands. "You can stay here and share Deanna's room but you have to go to school. Can you agree to that?"

I nodded, unable to speak. Emotion had stolen my voice. "Mom" gathered me into a hug and said, "It'll be all right, don't you worry now."

Deanna took me to her room where twin beds occupied opposite walls. I should have felt relief that I had somewhere to stay, but I didn't.

Days later, I saw Maggie at school. She walked right up to me and said, "Mom didn't kick you out. It was me. I'm sick of your crap. I told you to knock it off but you wouldn't listen."

Her words ripped through me. I folded my arms across my chest as numbness covered me like a shining suit of armor.

"Does she even know you did it?" I asked.

"She drove me to drop off your stuff, dumb ass, but I'm the one who did it," she said with power and pride in her voice.

Maggie's kicking me out was like swallowing razors, despite my pretense. All we ever had was each other, and now she had exiled me. *Screw her*, I thought bitterly. My stubborn pride prevented me from begging to come home. Instead, I rejected my family for rejecting me and I judged them for judging me. I set out to prove that I didn't need them. The fact that my mother had supported Maggie's decision was crushing.

She doesn't love me. She probably never did. I felt victimized, refusing to acknowledge that my lying and stealing had anything to do with the circumstance.

The truth was actually simple. My mother couldn't cope with me so she surrendered control to Maggie. She'd abandoned Karina in a similar way. I buried the rejection and hurt, hiding behind an ever-growing attitude of an, *I don't care, I don't need anyone* mantra. In my mind the only person who cared about me at all was Aaron.

I stayed with Deanna's family for the next five months. I attended school but I had a no idea how to function in a family unit. I was especially uncomfortable during meal times when the family sat together in the kitchen, talking about their lives and accomplishments. I felt I had nothing to offer. I didn't talk about Aaron because I knew others judged the relationship as inappropriate, because of our age difference. I didn't earn good grades in school, nor was I involved with any extracurricular activities. I never attended school functions like prom, homecoming, dances or sporting events. All of my free time was with Aaron and his friends or the few I had of my own.

During those five months, I spent most nights at Aaron's, returning to Deanna's for showers, trying to avoid meal times.

"So, when do you think you'll go back home?" Deanna asked one afternoon in her room while I folded laundry.

"Oh, I doubt I'll ever do that." I said. "They don' t want me there."

"Bummer. Well, when do you think you'll move out? I mean, you don't have to, but you can't stay here forever." I realized I'd stayed too long. We'd tried to be better friends and hang out together, but we didn't like the same things.

"I know. I'm sorry. You have been so cool. I'll find somewhere to go," I finished.

I knew I couldn't go home. I hadn't had contact with my family other than occasionally seeing, Maggie at school, but we never talked. I was desperately lonely and only felt loved when I was with Aaron.

School was nearly out and I had to find a place to live. What I'd discover next would mark a life-changing decision and resolve the question of where I would go.

THE MAN IN THE MASK—SWEETHEART RAPIST

Two women, Marcia and Sarah, sat sipping wine from bright red, plastic, cups in the front seat of Marcia's car. They liked each other and wanted a place to hang out and be alone. Fighting crowds or shouting over loud music at bars did not appeal to them. The secluded area of the defunct mines was perfect. It was a place notorious for lovers, aptly dubbed "Sweethearts Lane."

Both had a mild buzz—compliments of the sweet, white wine—when a bright light appeared through the driver's-side window, followed by a tap, tap, tap. Marcia was sure it was a cop as she rolled the window down.

The next thing she saw was a gun inches from her face. "Get out of the car and don't scream or I'll blow your head off," a man in a mask ordered.

The woman started hyperventilating and became overwhelmed with dizziness. *Calm, down, calm, down*, she told herself. The masked man forced her from the driver's seat and into the backseat of the car.

"Lay with your face down," he directed.

He removed his mask and pulled it over her face—the eyeholes at the back of her head. She could smell his vile odor in the stretchy fabric and gagged. Sarah was in the front, her body scrunched into a fetal position. Her face was pushed against the seatback and she desperately sucked air through the tiny gap. The gun was pointed at her head, while the man drove their car into a spot hidden from view.

"Don't look at me or I will have to shoot you, I'm going to join your friend in the backseat and if you so much as move, I will kill her first and you next."

"Oh-o-ha, o-kkay," Marcia stammered in between sobs. She was stunned and in shock. She couldn't get her thoughts together. Terror for her friend suffocated her and she didn't dare raise her head.

"Keep your head down and take your clothes off," the man ordered as he climbed back.

Marcia knew there was nothing she could do. Every word he spoke seared into her memory. She would never forget his smell, his voice or the inflection of his words—never.

Her skin crawled when he touched her. She tried to block out the smell and sensation when he forced his penis into her mouth, holding the gun to her head. She could hear Sarah's hysterical sobs, but something died inside when he touched her and she couldn't cry.

He finished by pushing himself inside her and she gritted her teeth as he tore the tender flesh, ripping deep into her very soul.

Afterward, the man felt good but could not admit the reason to himself. He shoved his dark actions away from his conscious mind. Instead, he began to whistle as he drove to the store to pick up items from his to-do list. He tucked the mask and gun under the front seat where he knew she would never look. Stupid bitch.

7

The room brightened by degrees. The sun burned through dark clouds and brought illumination one moment and muted softness the next. I swayed and twirled in sunlit circles. I held my arms around the swell of my belly and danced with childlike abandon. I tipped my head back and took a pull from the joint clutched tightly between my fingertips.

Just five months before, in the spring of 1978, I'd moved in with Aaron, who'd recently gotten his own tiny apartment, when I discovered I was pregnant. I was thrilled.

At sixteen, I wasn't concerned about the harm that smoking pot might bring to my precious unborn baby, a baby, I already loved and knew would love me more than anyone had ever dared.

I had no fear or worry about parenthood, only a single belief that neither classes nor instruction were needed for childbirth. I was swollen with the bright, youthful, arrogance of a teenager. I gazed upward and blew smoke, reflecting on the well-meaning people who'd offered unsolicited advice on the best way to birth a child. Complete strangers approached me in the supermarket and asked, "Are you taking Lamaze?" or, "Have you bought Dr. Spock yet? I couldn't live without it," they'd exclaim.

I thought, *they must not know that there are women in Africa, who squat and deliver their babies in fields every day and are just fine. Really!* I wanted to scream, *what's the big deal?* I gave no thought to suggestions of attending Lamaze classes and the popular book "Baby and Child Care" by Dr. Spock, was never purchased.

I was oblivious of what lay ahead. All that mattered was my unbridled joy for the baby I carried. *My baby will prove once and for all that I am worthy and capable. My baby will never suffer or go without, and I will never make him or her feel like a piece of crap. I will be the best mother in the world.* I couldn't imagine that my child would suffer for my immaturity, or that I couldn't give what I didn't have.

"I don't know what I'm going to do," I had said to Aaron one afternoon when it became clear that I needed to leave Deanna's house. "I have to find a place to go."

"You can move in with me." Aaron said, squeezing my hand. "I'll take you to school on my way to work. It'll work out."

I was ecstatic! He loves me! Finally, I can be happy. I moved in immediately.

I was scared to reveal my pregnancy to Aaron. I didn't want him to feel trapped, but I also didn't want him to reject us. I sat on the couch in our darkened living room biting my fingernails and rehearsing what I'd say.

I said nervously, "I'm pregnant, and I understand if you don't want to be involved, but I have decided to have this baby. Either way, I'm keeping it. I'll take care of the baby myself." I held my breath waiting for his reply.

"No," Aaron replied, "You won't have to do that. We'll figure it out. I love you and we'll be a family."

It was the first time he'd exclaimed his love outright. Relief swept through me. I wanted this baby and I wanted Aaron to want it too. The pregnancy was an opportunity to have a family of my own. I *knew* it was my destiny.

We found a small, two-bedroom house to rent that was affordable and close to the high school I attended. Aaron's mother agreed to loan us the deposit and Aaron's job as an auto mechanic would cover the rent and other expenses.

The house was in an old neighborhood where the sidewalks buckled and cracked under thick shade of the giant trees whose roots had effortlessly lifted the concrete. The front yard sprouted patches of green grass, while bushes under the windows were dried and brown with neglect. But it didn't matter. I was excited at the prospect of our very own home filled with things we would choose. I felt like a grown up.

"Oh, Aaron, look at the three windows in front, it will let in so much light. And look! It has a laundry room!" I exclaimed happily touring the house. *No more Laundromats,* I thought. "I love the kitchen too, don't you?"

"Yeah, it's a nice house. Hopefully we can get it." I felt Aaron's excitement and I was proud that it was me who could make him happy again.

We walked into the backyard, a graveyard of broken cement dividers and scattered rocks were strewn across an expanse of dirt and dried weeds.

I said, "It's not too bad. We can fix it up, right?" "Maybe, let's see if we can get it first."

I began my senior year of high school four months pregnant, walking the two blocks to school from our house. Now that I had a new life, I was determined to make everything perfect. The *light-body* was still present and I sometimes talked to it out loud, sharing my newfound happiness.

"Isn't this great? You must be happy now that I'm starting my family, right? This is what I'm supposed to do," I said with hopeful conviction.

But, I heard no reply, no voice in my mind, no response whatsoever. I was disappointed. I'd come to rely on the imagined approval I told myself the *light-body* gave. I didn't know what to expect but I'd hoped for something beyond silence. *I really am crazy,* I thought.

Daily retching started immediately in the mornings. I held my face inches from the toilet water, which splashed my bloodless face as streams of yellow bile, shot from my lips. The uncontrollable heaving came in waves and lasted most of the day.

There were no pregnancy tests at the local drug store yet. Affirming that you were pregnant required a blood test and gynecological exam. I scheduled an appointment that would confirm why I had morning sickness.

I lay exhausted, my feet resting in cold metal stirrups while the doctor probed with gloved fingers. The paper beneath me crackled with every breath. She snapped back the latex gloves dropping them into the built-in hole on the counter top, and answered my complaint, "It should stop in the second trimester. It usually does."

"Good. Because I'm sick all day. I've tried ginger ale and soda crackers and spearmint tea, but nothing works."

My mind raced back to that morning, bent over the toilet helpless in my heaves when Aaron bellowed, "Jesus Christ! Are you puking again? Hurry up! I need to shower!"

I told myself; He doesn't mean it. He's cranky in the mornings.

"I hope mine stops soon." I said to the doctor.

She replied, "If not, we can prescribe some pills that may help. There are new ones on the market." She almost smiled through her disapproval as she stepped out the door.

I got dressed beside the exam table and I thought, *please god, do this one thing and make it stop.* I looked for the *light-body* and spoke into the empty airless room, "Can't you do something?" But there was nothing there.

My baby was due in January. My plan was to have the baby during Christmas break and return to school at the end of that month. *It will be easy*, I thought. *No problem and perfect timing.* I was significantly unrealistic about what lay ahead.

The reality that living with Aaron was volatile and unpredictable slowly emerged. Aaron lost his temper at the slightest annoyance and smoked pot daily starting the moment he got out of bed.

"Where's my pot?" He demanded in a harsh voice as he looked up at me accusingly one morning.

"I think it's in the other room" I anxiously replied.

I hurried to retrieve the pot to avoid his explosive temper, returning seconds later holding the box aloft in front of my jutting belly. Before I reached him, I fumbled and dropped it. Tiny seeds, loose pot and a packet of rolling papers skittered out across the hard surface of the floor.

Aaron screamed, "You stupid cunt! What is wrong with you!?"

My heart began to pump in a hard rhythm. I hated the "c" word.

"Clean this crap up and you better hope, there's a joint in there!" he threatened.

"It was an accident, Aaron," I said, my tone sharp and defensive.

"You think money grows on trees? Christ," he retorted.

I scrambled to my knees and felt the cool, smooth, wood floor as I scooped the scattered debris with the edges of my hands. In my mind's eye I saw a flash of myself crawling on the floor and I felt ashamed. *How can I let him do this to me?* I agonized. Aaron got the broom and dustpan and threw them at me.

When his screaming and tantrums erupted, which could occur over the smallest incident, I took full responsibility. I chided myself for doing something to trigger his temper. He'd frequently say, "It's just that you make me so mad" or "If you would just stop nagging me, I wouldn't lose my temper."

I believed my actions controlled his. When he feels how much I love him, he will change. I knew deep down that his behavior would never change. He is who he will always be. You can't change him, the voice said.

No, I thought rejecting the voice and the knowing. He will change, I continually told myself. All he needs is someone to love him; he's had a hard life. He needs me.

Early in my third month of pregnancy my mother called. We hadn't talked since I'd been kicked out.

"Nita!" Aaron yelled after answering the phone. "It's your mom."

Surprised, I hurried to the phone clutching a can of Lemon Pledge. I'd sprayed it across the fake wood of our table, even though it didn't need it. I loved the smell. It was the first time in more months than I could count that I'd heard from my mother. I wondered if someone was hurt.

"Hello?" I said in an uncertain tone.

"Good morning, Nita," my mother said. "Are you all moved in?"

"Yeah, pretty much." I responded still skeptical. "How are you?"

"More importantly, how are you? I understand you're pregnant." I was sure Maggie told her.

"Yes," I chirped brightly. "I'm due in January." My pulse quickened, I knew my mother would not be happy. I tightened my grip on the phone, squeezed my eyes shut, and braced myself for her response.

"Are you sure this is what you want to do, Nita? You're pretty young to have a child. It's a lot of responsibility. How will you manage?"

"I've thought about it. I will be fine. I'll probably miss school for most of January but with Christmas break it should be all right. I should still graduate in June," I said with conviction.

"M-m-hm." Are you seeing a doctor? You're covered on my insurance you know. You are still a minor."

"Yes. I've been once. I go again next month. She gave me prenatal vitamins. They constipate me," I whispered, cupping my palm around the phone.

"Well, keep me posted," she said. "We had to move to the other side of town so come and see the new house. I have to get to work now, we'll talk later."

With that she hung up the phone. I was so happy my mother called and she didn't freak out about the baby. *This baby is making miracles already.*

In my sixth month of pregnancy Aaron and I drove to the grocery store. At a traffic light, a midnight blue Chevy Impala low rider, pulled beside us. Hugging the ground and sporting bright, chrome hubcaps polished to a mirror shine, it idled with a loud plap-plap-plap. I instinctively looked up and glanced into the car. Inside were four males. The driver was Hispanic and wore a thick bandana tied low over his forehead, his black hair shined with grease. Our eyes momentarily met. Aaron screamed, "You want to get out of the car and suck his dick you little whore!"

His accusation jolted and embarrassed me. His words stung like a slap. He threw the car into park and turned toward me.

"Just get out and give him a blow job! Get the hell out of my car," he screamed.

"No, Aaron, I didn't mean it. Stop it," I pleaded. I was squirming with mortification. *Where is this coming from?* I wondered.

"You get the hell out of my car right now!" His lips were wet with saliva and his eyes bulged from their sockets. He leaned across me and opened the car door and growled between gritted teeth. "Don't make me say it again."

Disgrace and humiliation were harder to bear than the exhaustive heat. I got out of the car and hurried into the neighborhood where no one could witness the shame of what I endured. Aaron sped from the light, his tires screeching and leaving a plume of smoke. I gave no thought to the filthy and degrading remarks that defined him. My ears were deaf to the sheer degradation and hateful tone in the nasty, unloving words that fell over me every day.

What did I do? I wondered all the way home.

By December, I'd stopped attending school. I couldn't get it together in the mornings. I was still plagued with severe morning sickness and nothing eliminated my constant nausea. I was thrilled, though, to have made up with my family. Maggie and I never talked about her kicking me out, but she had strong opinions regarding my decision to drop out of school.

"Don't drop out of school, you idiot. You'll be sorry. You'll have nothing. You have to get your high school diploma." Maggie looked at me sternly, disapproval apparent in her beautiful blue eyes.

"It'll be okay. Not everyone needs school. I don't even use the stupid stuff they teach you," I said, certain of myself.

In my seventh month, Maggie showed up at my house unannounced one afternoon,

"C'mon, I'll show you our new house," she said. "You'll like it."

"Okay," I eagerly agreed. I was excited to be included again and happy Maggie was back on my side. I'd missed her.

"Oh, my, god. What's going on?" I exclaimed as we entered the bright living room.

I saw my mother, Karina, and Isla smiling among many people crowded into the room. Colorful balloons filled the space and a large sheet cake decorated in "Winnie the Pooh" was proudly displayed on the table. The outpouring of love and support were overwhelming and unexpected. Karina lived a couple of hours away and I was shocked she was there. I received much-needed baby supplies and the day meant more to me than I could say.

I spent the days before the birth of my child frantically cleaning house. Like Milda, I wanted everything to be perfect and sparkling. Somehow, I'd tied my self-esteem and worth to how tidy I kept things.

I stood in the doorway and surveyed what would be the baby's room. A crib we picked up at a garage sale, newly-painted white, was filled with stuffed animals and a beautiful mobile hung over it. A changing table stocked with Johnson's baby shampoo, powder, and a stack of cloth diapers with pins and plastic pants filled the corner. Even though disposable diapers were all the rage, I wanted to do things the old-fashioned way. There was a tiny, plastic bathtub and small towels waiting for baby's first bath. I couldn't wait.

I read romance novels and watched soap operas to help pass the time and escape the reality of living with Aaron. I avoided the truth of my life and created my own reality.

The night I went into labor, the initial pain ebbed and came back just when I thought it was done. I shook Aaron awake.

"It's time to go. I think I'm in labor, for real this time." I mumbled.

There had been a false alarm with Braxton Hicks a few nights before and Aaron still resented having to lose sleep.

"Not now," he moaned. "I'm sleeping."

"Aaron, please, it hurts." My voice was strained and my tone unrecognizably high.

He didn't move or attempt to help me. Minutes passed and I tried again.

"Aaron, seriously, I need to go to the hospital."

"Jesus Christ!" he screamed. "I am tired and I need my sleep!"

Tears stung my eyes and I felt my throat constrict with rejection. He rolled away, turning his back to me.

"I'm having another contraction," I yelled. And then, I screamed, "OK, go to hell! Just go to hell, then!"

I rolled out of bed after the next contraction, staggered to the kitchen and called Maggie.

"Please, come and get me," I begged. "I'm in labor."

"Where's, Aaron?" she asked, groggy with sleep.

"He won't get up, Maggie, and I need to go"

"Okay, I'm coming."

When Maggie picked me up, she exclaimed, "What a jerk Aaron is. He's a total fuck up."

We arrived at the hospital after midnight and by two the next afternoon, I had not given birth nor had I dilated sufficiently. I was terrified and unable to relax. I was unprepared for the level of pain I felt. My mother and Maggie vigilantly stayed at my side.

An hour before I would finally deliver, I whispered, "Where's Aaron? Is he here?"

"No," my mother said. She was like an icy glacier when I said his name. "Don't worry, Nita, I'll come into the delivery room with you. You don't need him."

"Ok," I croaked. "You come in then."

Minutes before delivery, Aaron sauntered in, and announced that he was the father, and came into the delivery room. My mother waited in the hall. It was pure luck he arrived on time for the birth of his son. I swallowed the truth that Aaron abandoned us. I gulped down the knowledge that he was angry, abusive, and controlling. I dwelled in the fantasy of who I wanted him to be. I told myself that our son's presence would change him, because if you loved someone enough, and gave them precious gifts, they would change. I would forever regret not having my mother present for her first grandchild's birth.

In the moments after I gave birth to my son, I caught a glimpse, a flash in my mind's eye, of who I could be. A *picture* behind my eyes, showed a woman with a long braid and quiet determination. I felt her strength and *knowing*. It took several years to fully understand that my future self was born with my son.

At age seventeen, I held my beautiful son whom I named, Raine. After giving birth I felt like I had walked through a secret door into life. I was filled with awe. I breathed in the sweet scent of my boy and I whispered messages of love into his tiny ears. He gazed at me with beautiful, green eyes. He had what was called a "port wine" birthmark that looked like a tiny spill of red wine at the side of his face. From the beginning, I felt it made him unique.

Raine was a happy and agreeable baby never colicky or fussy. Nothing I had ever known was comparable to kissing his wet lips and open mouth while he smiled and watched me. Nothing at all.

Aaron's behavior worsened with the stress and demands of a new baby. His anger hovered like a poisonous fog around his body. I could no longer ignore his violent outbursts and filthy language in front of my precious Raine. Suddenly, my ears awakened and multiple realities dawned on me. I made a decision to leave.

"Mom, can Raine and I come live with you?" I said, to my mother on the phone. "I'm leaving Aaron. I can't take it anymore."

"Yes, come home," she replied without hesitation.

Although our relationship was strained, she was always there for me when it counted.

My mother doted over Raine and showered him with words of love and affection, something I never received from her. With Raine, she showed a gentler side of herself I hadn't known existed.

She'd say, "You're such a sweet, sweet, boy. You don't know how lucky you are Nita, to have such a sweet and easy child. None of you girls were as sweet as this baby."

Raine was six months old when I left his father. Aaron didn't try to stop me, but he told me I was on my own.

"Don't expect shit from me," he snarled. "You think you can do better. Go ahead, you stupid bitch."

After a couple of months passed, Aaron knocked on the door of my mother's house late in the evening. It was then I agreed to take a ride with him, and it was then that he made his first attempt to kill me, purposefully crashing his car into a ditch.

When Maggie picked me up from the twenty-four--hour store where I'd fled that night, my mother stared at me, her expression matter-of-fact. "Nita, you have to pull your head out of your ass. Aaron is a fuck-stick. He is angry and dangerous. He'll kill you if you give him a chance. Don't think he won't."

Why does everyone hate him? He was trying to scare me. He is harmless, I thought. I dismissed my mother's concern. I wanted to believe in the Aaron I'd created in my desperate need to be loved. I was accustomed to violence, anger, and hateful behavior as a normal expression of love. I blamed myself. I believed I brought out the worst in people.

It was past nine o' clock. When there were three loud raps at the front door. My mother opened it to find two officers standing on the porch.

"Good evening, ma'am," the tall one holding a flashlight said. "We're responding to a call about a suspicious person with a gas can tonight at this residence. In fact, ma' am, there is an odor of gas around the perimeter of the house and we found a discarded gas can on the east side of your home. Is there anyone you know, that may want to do you harm?"

The officer's partner was short and stocky with a large nose and barrel chest. His eyes darted suspiciously back and forth, scanning our living room while his partner talked. He reminded me of a bird dog searching for its prey.

"Do you mind if we come in and have a look around?" he asked, already stepping through the door.

"I know who did this," my mother fumed. "His name is Aaron Goddard and he is trying to kill my daughter." But without witnesses or fingerprints, the police would never prove it.

Goosebumps rushed over my skin. Shit. It couldn't be Aaron. But I knew that it was. I buried the knowing and prepared to defend him in my mind. Why, would Aaron endanger his own child? He wouldn't do that. No, it had to be a random incident, I rationalized.

Unbelievably, my mother called my father despite the late hour and their contentious relationship. I had no idea she even had his phone number. I stood in the hallway and did my best to eavesdrop on their conversation.

"Dell," my mother said sternly, "she needs a place to go and you are her goddamn father for Christ's sakes. For once, do something to help your daughter."

Things moved very quickly from that point on. It was decided—without any input from me, that I would immediately go to live with my father. Since I was only seventeen, baby or not, it seemed I had no choice in the matter.

SWEETHEART RAPIST—A FAMILY MAN

He was dubbed "The Sweetheart Rapist" by the media because the couples he attacked were in areas known for lovers. The man secretly savored the name, but he had a family now and was under a lot of pressure. Despite his love for them, his demons thumped beneath the surface. He felt weak. He yearned to take back his power and he knew just how to do it.

In the dark of the night, a couple walked hand-in-hand toward their car. It was late, but they'd wanted privacy and the caves were off the beaten track. They could be intimate there without being seen.

As the boyfriend dug in his pocket to retrieve his keys, a man suddenly appeared. He was wearing a ski mask and wielding a gun. "Give me your keys," he said, holding the gun inches from the boys head as he forced him into the trunk of the car.

"Get in and shut the fuck up." The masked man secured the trunk's latch.

"Get in the backseat and lay face down," he ordered the woman. Shaking and numb, she followed directions. Warm, stretchy fabric was pulled down over her head. "Oh no, please don't," she begged.

The boyfriend lay cramped and sweating in the trunk. Fumes of oily grit filled his lungs and soiled his thin t-shirt. He fumbled in the dark, searching for a weapon. He ground his teeth and imagined killing the man with his bare hands, when he got out of this suffocating trunk. He kicked violently with all his might and screamed, "Let me out you cowardly mother fucker! I 'm gonna kill you!"

He felt helpless as he heard the whimpers from the woman he loved as she was raped, only sheet metal between them, *Oh god, please, let me out so I can kill him.* He prayed, as tears of helpless rage rained down his face.

The Sweetheart Rapist took his time and raped the woman repeatedly in the backseat of the car. Afterwards he said, "Give me your driver's license."

The woman was in shock and moved like a puppet on strings. She retrieved her purse with stone hands. She'd disappeared somewhere inside of herself and escaped from the man and his vile breath. He studied her identification and handed it back.

"I'll come get you if you tell," the man said. "I know your name and I know where you live."

But the woman didn't hear him. She listened in her mind as her mother held her and sang a lullaby.

～

The woman came home late and found the house completely dark and quiet. She struggled through the doorway, her arms full of groceries. Something felt wrong. Her eyes searched the darkened room. She fumbled with the light switch as fear rushed through her. *What's the matter with me?* "Hey, honey, are you home?" she called. She walked to the living room, blood pounding in her temples. Dread generated a hard jolt in her chest, like an electric shock. "Are you here?" she called again, her voice quivering.

Something was in the middle of the room. Someone was there. Terror lodged itself like a swollen bean in her throat. She reached with quaking hands and turned the lamp on, nearly knocking it to the floor.

"Oh Christ, oh my god," she breathed. "What are you doing sitting here in the dark? What happened?" Her body tingled and she felt the weight of something dark and putrid hanging in the air.

The man smiled and said, "Nothing. Where have you been?"

8

I'd had no contact with my father since age twelve when he'd delivered Maggie and me on our mother's doorstep. Anxiety settled in my stomach, and I looked for the light-body but could not detect its presence. I'd come to rely on it as a sign that things would be all right. I wondered if it had abandoned me.

We were running from Aaron's hateful attempts to harm us.

Raine needed to be protected.

Hot, slippery tears stormed down my cheeks as I packed our belongings in a shiny, silver, footlocker. Its tomb-like smell ballooned in the room as I threw back the lid. I kept my head bowed while my mother talked.

"You're leaving in an hour. You'll be taken to your father's in Louisiana," she said, as she folded Raine's onesies and placed them in a neat, precise pile.

"Isla's boyfriend has a stepfather who owns a small plane and is willing to fly you and Raine tonight. You can't stay here, Nita. That scum bag will kill you and then I will have to have him put down, like the animal that he is and spend the rest of my life in prison."

"When did Dad move to Louisiana?" I asked in a voice heavy with gloom.

"I'm not sure. But he divorced Milda and is married to some other lucky woman. She has a couple of boys- just what your father always wanted."

I nodded. It shouldn't have surprised me, but the new information snaked through my body with a buzz. *What happened to Milda and her son Dickey? And who was my father married to now?* The questions fired in my mind but I didn't ask. I would find out soon enough. Sucking in air, I continued to pack our belongings. Raine slept peacefully through the entire ordeal.

"Is she ready?" came a man's voice from the living room.

I raised my forearm and wiped my snotty nose, grabbed an overstuffed diaper bag and slung it over my shoulder. I scooped up my sleeping son and walked numbly down the darkened hallway.

Stepping from the small plane, the hot, putrid, air that was Louisiana rose up in greeting, drenching my body in sweat. *Oh great. Humidity. That's just fantastic.* In the distance, I saw my father next to a pickup truck. He hurried toward the small two- engine plane and shouted, "Well h-e-l-l-o youngin." He reached out and laid his hand on my head and gently squeezed it. I held Raine protectively creating an instant barrier. "Go on and get in the truck, I'll be there shortly."

The truck sat idling, blasting cold air into the cab. I heard my father's voice as he loaded our trunk onto its bed, "I sure do thank y'all now. Y'all take care'n have a safe flight back on home," he chuckled.

My father looked the same. Stocky with blond hair and blue eyes, his face clean-shaven. He exuded a confident and a masculine air. I still believed he could do anything. Words escaped me as we drove in paralyzing silence for the first hour. Finally, my father finally spoke.

"So, you gone tell me what-in-the-hell-happened?" He glared.

His lips were thin and tight, reminding me of a turtle.

Those are Maggie's lips, I thought. "Mom thinks Aaron tried to set her house on fire," I said.

"Well, did he? Is that the son bitch that's this boy's daddy? I ain't heard nothing good 'bout him from nobody."

Fuck you. You think you know everything. Who have you been talking to? I thought to myself.

My father reached for his cigarette pack on the dashboard and lit a new one from the one he was smoking. Smoke hung like napalm around our heads. He threw the lit butt out the window with an angry flick of his fingers. Judgment glowed on his face like a hot ember.

"He's not that bad, and we don't know for sure if he did it or not," I said defensively.

"Didn't he just try to kill you, Nita? In a car the week before last or was your mother lyin to me? Ain't that enough? When you gone believe?"

"Yeah." I said exhausted, staring out the window as the road rushed by. *What does he know? He hasn't even met Aaron* , I thought as I dozed off.

I awoke with a start to the sound of shells crunching loudly under the truck's tires. A dingy white clapboard house, sat perched atop sturdy gray cinder blocks, unadorned and dismal. At some distance beyond it I saw a bright orange glow reflected off the water from the sunrise.

The tiny house looked desolate, surrounded only by a chain link fence and tiny broken shells. The repugnant smell of rotting fish accosted me as I stepped from the cab. Disillusionment throbbed within me. *This can't be where he lives,* I thought. *Oh please, God, it can't be.*

"Go on in. The doors ain't locked," my father grunted, lifting our trunk over the tailgate.

Yeah, because who would steal from this shit hole. How can you live here? I thought belligerently as I opened the door.

The floor was covered in shabby, faded, linoleum tiles. The distinct odor of fried fish saturated the humid air inside. My heart sank at the squalor. The living area opened to a drab kitchen. The sink was filled with dirty dishes and on the counter sat a deep-fryer with an abandoned wire, mesh basket, lying on its side over grease-soaked paper towels. In the hallway stood a tall woman with strawberry-blonde hair and on the couch, two boys sat at opposite ends.

"Hi," I said.

She spoke slowly. "Hi there. Y'all must be tired. I'm Della'Rae and this here is Harry and Neil, my boys."

She talked like she was on vacation—slow and leisurely. Della'Rae was pretty. She was tall and lean, with blue eyes and an easy smile. Harry, the oldest boy, had longish, dirty blond hair, with blue eyes and sculpted masculine features. He was very handsome and only slightly younger than I was. Neil, the younger, brother, had the same hair as his mother and was two years younger than Harry. Neither boy spoke. I felt an instant connection with Harry, which helped me relax and not feel so out of place. The new sleeping quarters for Raine and me would be on the fold-out couch in the front room. The first few days were awkward and my hostile, adolescent attitude was in full bloom.

I was told that my father owned a tug-boat business. I couldn't understand why he would live in an isolated, shabby, little house on cinder blocks at what felt like poverty central. It was depressing and bleak. My mother had no money and we were frequently on welfare, but we never lived like this.

Harry and I bonded right away. We sat on the steps in front of the house later that day, commiserating.

"Want a cigarette?" he offered.

"Definitely, thanks. Harry, what is that disgusting smell?" I asked wrinkling my nose.

"Oh, it's the Pouge plant next door. Little fuckin fish made into cat food and shit. Fuckin stinks don't it?"

"It is the most disgusting smell ever. I don't know how you live here."

"Yeah, well neither do I. It sure ain't my choice. So, yurr Dell's daughter huh? He don't never talk about y'all. He's just an asshole most of the time."

"Really? What's he do?" I asked blowing smoke.

"Oh, he's just on my ass, day and night. I work with him on the boat. Bout the only thing I can say is, he works hard. He ain't no slouch. But that's it. That's all he's good for," he chuckled glancing at me he smiled, lighting his handsome face and said, "Otherwise he's an asshole."

"Wow, that's too bad," I replied. I'm not sure why, but hearing that about my father, surprised and disturbed me.

I liked Della'Rae, who was easy-going and kind. She helped me with Raine, and genuinely enjoyed having him there. That first day, she'd reached out her arms and wiggled her fingers cooing, "Can I take 'im? Oh he's so precious, aren't you, sweet boy."

She snuggled close, breathing in the scent of my son. She placed him on her hip and said, "You wanna come with Della'Rae and see sumthin fun? C'mon. I'll show you sumthin." And she sashayed down the hall disappearing into her bedroom.

I turned eighteen the month after I'd arrived, the legal drinking age. My father knew the owners of an upscale restaurant in town and arranged an interview for me. I was hired and started working most nights as a cocktail waitress. I didn't drink alcohol—I hated it—but serving it was lucrative.

Della'Rae babysat temporarily, but my father pressured me to make other permanent childcare arrangements. It was tense between us. He didn't know how to be a father and I didn't know how to be a daughter.

I didn't cook or clean what I considered to be a "shit hole." I rarely made my bed on the fold- out couch and I only added to Della'Rae's laundry. I never offered to help and I was oblivious to anyone's needs except my own.

I had a bad attitude and no respect. I didn't know that I should wrap soiled diapers in a plastic bag, before discarding them. I simply threw them in the trash, which I didn't empty. No one said a word to me about my habits until my father exploded one morning out of nowhere.

He screamed, "This house smells like baby shit! It's a stinking outhouse in here! You just throw them dirty diapers in the trash for all of us to smell! Are you a goddamned pig?"

"What do you want me to do with the fucking diapers?!" I screamed back.

He slapped me across my face, knocking me backward and jumped on me, pinning me to the unmade bed of the fold-out couch.

"You better clean up your filthy mouth, little girl. You don't swear in my house, you hear me?"

"Fuck you! This house is a pigsty! A shit hole. How can I possibly make it worse?"

He held me down and we struggled until Della'Rae yelled, "Stop it, Dell, that's enough now. Get off her!"

"You better pack your shit and find somewhere else to go! We have had enough of your ungrateful attitude!" he roared.

My father watched me gather our few meager belongings, pushed a wad of cash in my hands, and dropped Raine and me at the restaurant where I worked. It wasn't even noon, as I stood defiant and full of anger. I flipped my father the bird as he drove off, leaving us in an empty parking lot with nowhere to go.

We moved in that afternoon with Lana, a waitress who worked with me. She'd lost her mother only months before, leaving her alone with two siblings. The three of them lived together in the family home, but their lives were in turmoil. Lana' s younger brother was in middle school, her older sister, in her first year of college and Lana, had just graduated from high school. The house was only two blocks from the restaurant so we could walk to and from work.

I felt their mother's presence in the house constantly, and occasionally, she talked to me. I heard her in the same manner that I heard the *voice*.

"Things are a struggle for them. I know they're sad and lonely. Lana is the strong one though, and she'll see to her brother and sister. She was always the most level headed," she told me.

Lana told me her mom died of breast cancer and I felt the suffering of the family before her death.

A picture in my mind showed me a woman, frail and bony lying in bed. I could smell her death as she lay helpless, slipping away.

Sadness and disbelief floated in the air between her children as they waited for the inevitable.

I would catch glimpses of her standing in the kitchen, or walking through a room. It seemed she was everywhere.

I knew Lana's older sister would drop out of college and her little brother would lose his way too, drowning in grief with nowhere to turn. Loss was a living thing in their house, and it weighed heavily on me. I had no idea what to do when I heard or saw their mother, so I told myself I was imagining things and stayed silent.

Out of the blue, my father called me at work a month later. "I got y'all a trailer down on the bayou across from the Les Bonton Roulet. It has furniture and some food to get y'all started. The keys for it are at the bar. Ask for Annie, she'll give um to ya. You can pay me the rent next month."

"Ok, Dad, thanks." I said surprised. "I'll check it out after work."

Neither of us apologized or mentioned our fight.

Though I was grateful for Lana's kindness, I couldn't breathe in a house filled with so much pain. I moved into the trailer alone with Raine. My father and I had little contact except at the end of the month when I paid him my rent. We never engaged in conversation.

I was lonely and isolated with no phone, TV, or neighbors. Across the street from our trailer was a bar and literally nothing else for miles. Harry was my only visitor, but being sixteen, he had little time to come and see me. We'd become friends and allies and genuinely liked one another.

"When you go back to California, I'm comin too. Soon as I turn eighteen, we'll go together. We can share an apartment. I always wanted to see California," Harry said.

"Okay. When you turn eighteen. The girls will love you there. You look like a surfer boy."

After a few months, plagued with loneliness, I moved again, this time into a small apartment in town.

I quickly discovered that I could earn more money bartending than cocktailing. I lied about my lack of experience and landed a job at Pat O' Brien's, in New Orleans, a popular nightspot and home of the famous, "Hurricane." The head bartender knew in minutes that I had no experience, but instead of ratting me out, she took me under her wing.

New Orleans was an hour and half commute, so I'd pack up Raine and searched for a sitter and a place to stay almost nightly. We would sleep on floors or couches or anywhere I could find. It didn't take long to realize the situation was untenable, so I quit my job and looked for one in the town where I lived.

A giant black and gold sign that read "Gold Rush" flashed in front of a stand-alone building on the corner of a busy thoroughfare. At 10:30 in the morning the bar was closed, but I pulled the heavy wooden door open, balancing Raine on my hip, hoping someone was hiring inside. Stale cigarette smoke clung to the walls and mixed with the soured smell of spilled beer and stinking urine. As my eyes adjusted to the darkened room, I saw two pool tables side-by-side to my left, and scattered tables and chairs to my right. A long bar made of battered wood stretched out in front of me. Behind the bar, counting money from an open cash register was a tall man in a black t-shirt and skin-tight jeans. Beside him was an older woman with pasty skin that reminded me of a dead reptile bloating in the sun. She was nearly bald and I could see that her hands shook badly.

"Excuse me. I'm looking for the person who hires people. I'm looking for a job."

"Is that right? What kind of job you lookin for, hon?" the man asked.

"A bartending job," I replied.

"Well, hon, I'm Ronnie and this is Dora. She owns the place. I just help out, right, baby?" He kissed her forehead, tenderly. "We ain't lookin' for no nighttime bartender but we need someone to clean the bar in the mornin', that means floors, bathrooms and tables and get the bar set up for the night. We do a little lunch business too. You'd have to start day shift first; then we'll see what comes."

"Okay. I'll take it. I'm looking for childcare too, do you know anyone?"

The woman spoke for the first time. "My cousin lives just off

Grand Caillou Road and she has a daycare. Ronnie'll give you her number."

I started two days later cleaning the bar from the night before and tending bar all day. The smell of the Gold Dust in the morning was like licking the bottom of an ashtray, rinsing with urine, and washing it down with stale beer. I tried everything to block the offending odor, from rubbing Vicks Vapo Rub under my nose to holding my breath and running outside gasping for air, but nothing worked.

Fortunately, I moved to the night shift after a couple of months. I made so much money, I didn't know what to do with it. I hid one hundred-dollar bills inside my socks and stuffed them deep in my dresser drawers.

I met a crowd who partied and I quickly fell back into the drug scene, leaving Raine night after night at childcare. Dora's cousin who'd babysat during the day was willing to keep Raine overnight. In the beginning, I'd pick him up at three a.m. after work, but it wasn't long before I didn't pick him up for a couple of days. I don't know why the woman never reported me to child services.

I thought running from Aaron would change things for Raine and me, but it turned out, I was the same frightened, insecure girl with no self-esteem. I was easily lured back into the destructive behavior I was used to. I became a danger to my precious Raine.

I had no contact with my father and seldom spoke to anyone in my family, including Maggie.

Months later when she came to visit our dad, and to see me, I avoided her. I didn't want her to judge my life, although at the time, my excuses of "being too busy" seemed valid. Finally, after Maggie's persistent nagging, we spent the last couple of nights together. She pleaded with me to come home.

"Nita, come back with me. Come home. You need help with Raine and you party too much."

I looked at her sideways as I drove. "No, way. I'm not going. Raine is fine, don't worry about it."

"You party every night, Nita. You look like shit and so does Raine. You need to stop."

"Don't get all high and mighty, Maggie. Like you don't party too."

"I don't have a kid."

"Whatever," I fired back. But Maggie didn't let up. Instead, she changed tactic saying,

"Just let me take Raine back with me. Just for a while."

"No, fucking way, Maggie!" I said angrily. "I'm his mother and he needs me. He stays here."

"He needs someone to take care of him." Maggie said. "Forget it." I finished.

We pulled up in front of a lone trailer that had rust stains dripping like paint from its roof.

"Wait here," I said to Maggie, "I'll be right back." Cicadas sang their nighttime songs and the air, thick with moisture, saturated my skin. I went inside, eager to get my fix quickly, but after several minutes passed, Maggie became impatient and threw open the trailer door.

"Hey, hey, now. Who's this here? You just walk into someone's home, baby?" said Hollywood.

Hollywood was my contact for everything intravenous and was willing to shoot me up. I still couldn't do it myself. He was tall and blond with delicate features that belonged on a woman. His face was clean-shaven, dimpled, and his chin had a deep cleft. You would think women would swoon over him, but he was more feminine than masculine. We all thought he looked like a movie star which is how he earned his name.

My arm lay across Hollywood's lap. I held the end of a belt, black and cracked with age, tight over my bicep. The hard metal buckle bit into my arm, squeezing doughy flesh through its tiny openings. Hollywood had emptied the syringe into my vein just as Maggie barged in.

"Oh- my- god, Nita! What the hell are you doing?!" Maggie screamed. "Oh, my, god, you are totally screwed up. Take me back to the hotel. You are disgusting!"

Neither of us spoke on the way to the hotel where Maggie was staying. Her disapproval and disgust was visceral and bounced around in the car. It consumed anything that was ever good between us.

"I can't believe how fucked up you are, Nita. Please, let me take Raine with me." Maggie pleaded.

"No way, Maggie. Raine, stays put. I don't do it all the time. Lighten up."

"Oh my God, You are so messed up."

The next morning, piercing cries pulled me out of a dead sleep. Raine had somehow escaped from the confines of his crib and stood at the foot of my bed, clutching a bottle in his little fist. I glanced at the clock beside me, it was eleven a.m. I saw thick, yellow custard float on clear water through the bottle's milky plastic.

My son's chest was bare, showing an outline of ribs as he sucked in air. A diaper, heavy with urine, hung from his bottom nearly dragging on the floor. His face was red and dirty and his eyes brimmed with sadness instead of tears. Anger boomed across his sweet, red lips. A single tooth jutted from his top gum and I couldn't remember its coming. In that instant, I saw retched neglect clinging to my child like a fever. Had I really sunken so low?

"Oh my god," I cried, "Oh my god." I leapt out of bed. Regret and shame pounded through my veins. *Jesus Christ*. I thought. *What have I become?* I saw my failure, gross and unthinkable. The knowledge bloomed like a hideous vine that choked my very soul.

I had been living in a constant state of denial and escape, just as I had with Aaron. I was nineteen and my beautiful Raine was eighteen months.

When I awoke to my son's painful cries that morning, I saw myself through Maggie's eyes. I witnessed my utter neglect. Before picking Maggie up to drop her at the airport, I called my mother.

I gripped the phone with sweaty palms and pressed it tightly to my ear, "Mom, I need help."

"What's wrong? Are you ok?" she asked with alarm in her voice.

"I can't take care of Raine. I'm tired and can't get up in the morning and...." I tried to force words through the knot in my throat. "He's hungry and, I'm a bad mother. I'm neglecting him and he needs someone," I sobbed. "He has his top tooth and I don't remember when he got it."

"Alright, Nita, calm down and get a grip. I'll help you. Send Raine to me. Is Maggie still there?"

"Yes."

"He can come back with Maggie," she said.

I fed Raine and drew him a bath and faced the evidence of my life. I discovered a flaking skin condition on Raine's scalp and his crib reeked of dirty sheets, soiled diapers and soured milk. *How does he get out of this crib?* A pile of unwashed clothes sat in a filthy heap in a corner of his room. My refrigerator was empty and I looked like shit. I was deep in the throes of addiction. I was lost.

At the last minute at the airport, I handed Raine, over to Maggie.

"Oh, thank god. You're doing the right thing." She disappeared down the jet way with my son.

It was crushing to realize my failure, but I felt powerless to change my situation. I hadn't yet admitted that I was an addict. *I'll stop doing drugs tomorrow or this will be my last time,* I told myself every day. And I believed it.

I felt free for the first time since the age of sixteen. I was almost nineteen and I didn't think I would miss my son but I was wrong. Everywhere I looked I saw Raine. I longed for him so badly that my stomach cramped and my breasts throbbed as though they were filled with milk.

Mothers and their smiling children were everywhere. The supermarket, gas stations, restaurants, and streets. *Why can't I do that? Why can't I be a good mother?* After giving my baby to Maggie, I did what addicts do and indulged in more drugs, drowning in self-pity and shame. The behavior lasted only a few weeks more before I overdosed again.

THE SWEETHEART RAPIST GETS PRACTICE

The couple kissed intimately and caressed each other, their bodies buzzing with what lovers want. They embraced on the car's long front seat, squeezed together in desire. It was dark and private, and the windows steamed with the evidence of their passion.

Headlights, harsh and bright, sliced through the rear windshield and seconds later came a tap-tap-tap at the passenger's side window. The woman rolled the window down, afraid it was the police. She drew back and gasped at the gun barrel inches from her face.

The man in the mask's adrenaline was in high gear and his breath was ragged. Without hesitation, he reached in and grabbed the women firmly by her hair and ordered her to open the car door.

"Don't scream," he warned as he held his gun to her head. "I'll shoot you." He barked at the man who, only moments ago, was swollen with lust.

"Get out, and get in the trunk or I will kill her."

"No way man," the startled lover replied. "I'm not gonna do that."

The man in the mask, fired a shot that whizzed over the woman's head, and placed the gun's snout firmly against her temple and said, "She's next."

"Okay, okay, man. Take it easy," the young lover, who was now scared shitless, responded.

"Open the trunk and get in," the man in the mask ordered. "Don't fuck with me, buddy, I will kill you both. Now get in," he repeated.

As her boyfriend climbed in the trunk, the woman's chest heaved and she could not control herself. She knew what was coming and she began to plead. "Oh p-please, let me go. Oh god. Please don't," she said as warm urine ballooned in her jeans.

9

The smell of decay, rotting food, and stale tobacco went unnoticed as I lay unconscious on the backseat of my car. Dumped like a sick pet by my drug-wielding friends, I lingered alone in the dark.

I'd shot up with a drug called Dilaudid, a painkiller stronger than morphine. It marched through my veins like a malicious army. Unable to move or speak, my body shuddered involuntarily with dry heaves. The side of my face was slick with thick, gummy spit and my eyes were glazed at half-mast. I panted like an overheated animal. I observed all of this from the top of the car.

Out of my body, I felt acceptance rather than anxiety for my physical state. I understood a number of things at once. I could leave my body and life behind in what we call death, or return to it and move forward. I also understood that if I left my body, I would simply go on. It wouldn't be the end of me.

There was no right or wrong, simply a choice. I was aware of sounds or vibrations, not from my physical world but from the light in which I floated. It pulsed and danced with life even though I had no body. I experienced an odd pull to float further into the light, away from my body that lay sick and dying in my car.

What I experienced that day was and is difficult to explain. I felt and understood multiple truths, though no words were ever spoken. I had gone out of my body and overdosed before, but I had not experienced this. I *knew* a choice had to be made, of this there was no question.

It was the light and love of my son that drew me back to my body. The deep awareness that I had so much more to do, kept me in this world. I'd made the decision to live and to heal. When I returned to my body, I was sick but I *knew* I would pull through. I *knew* I was finished with drugs. It was like I took off a coat that no longer fit and left it behind. For me, what I underwent changed everything. With a brief exception a few years later, I never used drugs again. I'd made a decision to get sober and when I did, I called my mother.

"Hi Mom, how's Raine?" I asked with a clear voice.

"He's good; he's such a sweet boy. Isla has him most of the time because my work schedule has changed."

"I can come and get him. I'm ready." There was silence on the line before she said;

"It's only been a few weeks Nita. I don't think it's a good idea."

"But, I'm ready and I want him back. He's my son. I need him." I said, my voice cracking with emotion.

"That's fine, but I need some proof that things are different. I can't let that sweet boy be mistreated again."

Giant tears spilled from my eyes, so heavy with regret, they scarcely touched my cheeks before splashing into my lap. "What do I have to do mom, how can I prove it?"

We agreed that I must have a clean place to live, a steady job, and complete some classes at a community college. And no more drugs. I could have Raine if I did this for three months.

Three months later, I flew back to California, driving straight to Isla's to pick up Raine. Maggie was furious, screaming on the phone, "You don't deserve him. I'll fight you in court for him. I won't let you have him."

It would destroy our relationship for years. But Maggie let go and prayed I'd stay sober.

I pulled open the screen door at Isla's house and let it slam behind me. I could hear Raine giggling from another room and I was exploding with silly excitement. I clutched a stuffed animal I'd brought for him and knelt down, waiting for my son to see me and run into my arms.

Raine looked at me as though I were a complete stranger. He walked warily past me twisting a ball between his little hands as he glanced sideways in my direction. My stomach twisted, my smile fell away. I'd lost my son. I sat numbly on the couch, the ethos of my neglect settling around me in a thick stink.

Isla said "It'll be alright. He just needs some time."

I waited, choking on tears and self- judgment. I would struggle with that moment for years and blame myself for every stumble Raine encountered during his young life. Eventually, Raine crawled tentatively into my lap and I held my child, hoping for forgiveness one day. It would take years for me to understand that I had to forgive myself too.

I returned to Louisiana with Raine and a newfound determination. But I was alone and vulnerable, terrified to make another mistake. I needed help and I believed I couldn't ask my family. Late one night, I sat staring at my phone. I picked it up and called Aaron.

"Nita, I'm so glad you called. I've been waiting and hoping you'd call. I've changed. I really have. Just give me a chance. I love you and I want my family back. You're the best thing I've ever had, let me prove it," he begged. "I have a good job and I can take care of us if you'll come home."

I wanted to believe him. I needed to believe him. I was afraid of failure, and the realities of single parenting with no support or help weighed heavily on me. We began to talk a couple of times a week. At Aaron's request, I'd hold the phone to Raine's ear, "Hey, little man. It's Daddy. You know how much I miss you? Hey, I bought you some cars we can play with when you come home, would you like that?"

Raine's face would light up when he heard Aaron's voice and it broke my heart. Guilt set in. I was denying my son his father.

I began to remember the good things, the sweet things about

Aaron. I pushed the rest aside and prayed he'd really changed. I owed it to Raine to try again. So, in a few weeks, convinced I was doing the right thing, Aaron flew to Louisiana, packed us up and we drove west.

One afternoon, after running errands, I walked in to the house to Raine's screams rolling down the hall. I rushed to his room. Aaron held Raine on the floor and each time he struggled upright, Aaron pushed him back down, laughing. "C'mon, little man, you can't get up? C'mon, try again."

Raine screamed, red-faced, in angry frustration.

"Aaron! Let him up! Stop holding him down! It's not funny. He's just a little boy!" I scooped Raine from the floor. "It's ok, baby," I cooed, wiping the tears from his face.

Hatred for Aaron exploded in my chest. His cruelty could no longer be ignored.

When Raine toddled determinedly across the floor, Aaron would trip him and laugh at his fall. He'd reach out randomly and thump on his head. I wanted to kill Aaron when I saw his malicious acts against our son.

It was clear that Aaron had not changed, and I regretted moving back in with him. Two months after our return, I was pregnant again. My family was disgusted with my decision to return to a volatile and abusive relationship. *I am twenty years old and on baby number two,* I thought.

My mind flashed back to the *pictures* I'd seen when I was eight of the two women (that as it turned out, I knew from high school) and their conversation. I was stung with the truth of the vision. *I have to abort this pregnancy, I can't have another baby,* I thought. I made an appointment at a women's clinic.

I dropped Raine off with my mother and as I made my way out the door she said, "This baby is meant to be, and if you abort her, she will find a way into your life. It's a mistake Nita, and you will regret it for the rest of your life."

And there it was, her *knowing*. My mother almost never interfered in my life and her statement made a powerful impact.

Crap, I thought as I walked out the door. *How does she know it's a girl?* I drove to the clinic and sat in a hard, blue, plastic chair while my stomach churned and the voice warned me. *She's right, it's a mistake. The child is yours and waits for you.*

"Nita," the nurse called from the inner door. I quietly gathered my things and left. For the next eight months I tried to bury my dread. I carried a child I falsely believed I didn't want. I felt helpless and trapped. I waited for my daughter's birth and I did not suspect she would change my life the instant I gazed into her pale, blue eyes.

Elizabeth had a light that astonished me, and all my anxiety and fear melted away when I saw her. She was beautiful, with smooth skin and pink cheeks, blonde, hair and sky-blue eyes. I felt inner strength radiate from her tiny body and *knew* that now my family was complete. I had to find a way to leave Aaron, I just wasn't sure how. I was eternally grateful for my mother's insight.

Aaron's behavior was unnerving and his actions had become increasingly erratic. He'd sauntered in one afternoon and casually related what had occurred only moments before. "Some stupid bitch cut me off on the freeway. So, I sped up and passed the bitch and then got in her lane and slammed on my brakes and backed up. The bitch barely missed me! She probably pissed her pants!" he laughed.

"What is wrong with you, Aaron? People don't do things like that. You have a serious problem. You're sick," I said, horrified and clutching Elizabeth to my chest.

I have to get away from him. I have to make him so mad, so disgusted with me, he will kick me out. Then it will be his decision. Maybe, if he hates me, he will leave me alone, and want nothing more to do with me and I will be free. My thoughts ran wild with scheme after scheme. I was afraid of Aaron and unable to stand in my truth and say, "I don't love you and I want out." A plan took shape in my mind. I would have a one-night stand so he would hate me for cheating, something he accused me of regularly. I convinced myself that was the only answer.

I arranged a ski trip to Tahoe with a girlfriend for a week, and left my children with Isla. Elizabeth was just five weeks old. My plan was simple, cheat on Aaron, admit it, and then let him kick us out.

As soon as we arrived in Tahoe, we went straight to a bar where a band was playing. I spent the night with the lead guitarist. The experience was empty and sad.

On the drive home, uncertainty of my plan grew and choked any resolve that I'd had. My hands began to sweat and my mouth turned dry. I couldn't imagine what Aaron would do.

Immediately when I stepped through the threshold of our home, accusations of infidelity flew like daggers from Aaron's tongue. I denied such behavior and my chance to escape was washed clean away. I put the children to bed for the night and Aaron's filthy monikers raged on.

"I know you fucked somebody!" he screeched. "You're a whore and always have been!"

I stood silently. Just say it, I thought, tell him he's right, let him kick me out.

"I did it," I blurted. "I'm sorry but I had an affair, I did it."

My insides felt like putty as I waited for his response. Aaron scowled at me.

"You fucking bitch, I knew it," he screamed. "Just say, I'm a fucking whore." His eyes were wild and he grabbed the hair at the back of my head and forced me down the hall to our bedroom. He pushed my face into the mirror,

"I am a fucking whore!" he screamed, "Say it! I am a nasty, dirty, stinking, fucking whore!" he went on. "Now say it, bitch, say it!"

I was stunned. *"Please god, please, don't let the children wake up,* I prayed. My teeth chattered and my body shook as though I were in a snowstorm. I whispered, "Please, p-p-p-please, Aaron, d- d-don't w-wake the children. Sh-sh-sh-sh."

"I said say it!" He bellowed louder than ever. "O-k-kay, I'm a whore," I choked.

"No, stupid! I'm a dirty, fucking, whore!" and he pushed my face against the cold-mirrored glass. Spit and snot smeared my reflection and my mouth was gaping. My lip began to bleed, spreading a pink tint across the mirror and my gums.

"I a-a-m a d-d-dirty, f-f-fucking whore," I breathed. My mind raced as I listened for the slightest noise or cough. My ears attuned for my children's cries. Thank God there were none.

Aaron's hateful breath assaulted my face. I felt his rage as I was forced to inhale his toxic and broken soul. He tore at my clothes and chanted vile sentiments like a man possessed. He threw me on the bed and I plunged downward with the water that filled it. He held my face in his hand, squeezing the soft pallet of my cheeks together, his fingers nearly touching. His knee was planted firmly on my chest. He held himself in one hand masturbating furiously, and although he was unable to grow hard, he still expelled his sickness on my face.

"That's how whores like it," he groaned.

I felt such shock, such repulsion. A fire drill screeched in my mind- evacuate evacuate, it trilled and I did. Like a guilty marauder I fled the scene from my conscious mind, leaving my body to witness and be the keeper of all that came after, alone and abandoned. I retreated to a desolate mental cage cowering and afraid. It was as if I'd never known him, as he pushed inside me, ripping and tearing innocent flesh.

There was no tenderness in his hands, only a disgusting depravity that burrowed like flesh eating weevils into my skin. I held no concept of time as he raped and bruised my body the hours flew.

At some point during the night, I found myself naked and huddled against the rough stucco wall outside of the duplex where we lived. I didn't feel the cold, although I saw my breath. I had no recollection of how I'd gotten there. The porch light blazed and I pleaded through swollen lips, "Please, Aaron, please let me in. I'm sorry, pleeease, Aaron." Finally, he did.

My frame of reference after I came inside is vague at best, but eventually Aaron was spent and he lay beside me asleep. I inched carefully and quietly from the prison of water to the floor. I knew Aaron had a rifle high on a shelf in the closet I drove myself forward until I sat naked and shivering on the closet floor. I held my breath and fantasized of how I would shoot him.

"Can you kill him?" a voice whispered. *I wondered then, Is the gun*

loaded, and if not where are the bullets and how do I load them without waking him? What will become of my children if he awakens and kills me?

I abandoned my fantasy and crawled on hands and knees down the hall, sick with the reality that I could not kill him. I wrapped myself in a bed sheet from the hallway linen closet and tried in vain to wipe away his fury that dripped like acid down my thighs. I waited- - my body tucked inward like a child, scarcely breathing- for him to awake and my mind took me back to a memory from six months before this nightmare began.

A *light-body* had materialized before my eyes. Its vibration rattled my insides like I had just stepped off a train. I was not afraid and I recognized that this *light-body* was different from the one I was familiar with. *Pictures* behind my eyes began, along with the *knowing* and I saw a very old Chinese man with skin that looked like leather and hung from his bony arms. My body felt the hunger that filled his empty belly. He walked bent with the weight of loss on his shoulders. Tied to a tether he held was a mule, so skinny that the bones of its flanks stuck up like fins. In his dark and desolate eyes I saw the whole of his life. Who he had been as a young man was clear, and I experienced the wisdom and pain that lived within him. In that moment, I felt our oneness. It was otherworldly.

There were no words spoken, but I *knew* the *light-body* before me had been the old man in a past life. I *knew* that he had lived countless other lives too, although I held no knowledge of past-life ideology. I knew the *light-body* was connected with Raine to guide him or teach him. They were part of each other, we all were but I wasn't sure how. *"It's time to go now"* he said without speaking. *"To stay changes life path and soul intent. It's time to go."*

I *knew* that Raine's life choices and mine were intertwined and unbreakable. The baby inside of me kicked as if to say, *Do you get it?* I understood the message, but I was afraid to make a change. The *light-body,* like all I had encountered in the past, emanated loving steady energy. In moments it was gone, leaving me with more questions than answers.

Crap, I thought, coming back to the present moment, *What am I going to do?* I *knew* I had to leave Aaron, but I was afraid of what he might do.

He will never let me go. I'd been struggling daily to hide my growing anxiety, fear, and disgust. It was the reason that I'd formed my plan to escape.

Noise, from the bedroom meant Aaron was awake. He got up and left for work like it was a normal day. I pretended to be asleep, but feared he would see the hard pulse of my heart, move with the sheet that covered me. He never came near the couch where I lay wrapped like a mummy. Immediately after he left I woke the children, got dressed, and called Isla. "Isla, it's me. Can you come get me?"

"What's wrong? Is something wrong?"

"Yes, something is wrong. You have to come get us, right away. I'm leaving Aaron. He's gone over the edge. It's for good this time, I swear. Please, Isla hurry. I know he'll come back and try to stop me."

"Okay, let me get gas and I'll bring the van. I should be there in an hour."

"Thank you, Isla."

In a frantic dash I shoved all I could into giant green trash bags and pushed the horrors of the last night from my mind. When Isla arrived, we quickly carried everything to the van.

Suspecting my departure, Aaron left work and returned home. I had just fastened Elizabeth into her car seat when he pulled in the drive. "Where do you think you're going?" He spat.

"I'm leaving, Aaron, and you can't stop me." I ran back into the house to get my purse and one last bag. Isla had called the police from a neighbor's phone the minute she'd seen him.

"You think you can do anything you want?" he hissed. Aaron spun violently around and I watched his anger form in hostile circles of rage. Spotting the broom tucked between the refrigerator and kitchen counter, he grabbed it, turning the wooden handle into a weapon. He swung wildly and shattered my beloved houseplants. I stood immobile and watched the dirt and clay rain down like exploding grenades.

"You think you can just leave?" Sweating and red-faced he

dropped the broom and went to our bedroom to retrieve his rifle, brandishing it like a sword.

"I'd rather shoot you," he said in a choked and broken voice.

His eyes filled with tears.

"The police are coming," Isla called from outside.

Aaron looked away and regained his composer. He slid the glass door open calling to our neighbor who stood on his back porch, eavesdropping. "Hey, buddy, can you hold this for me?" he asked as he handed his illegal firearm over the fence. I couldn't believe the gall of our neighbor, whom I never laid eyes on. The officers arrived and separated us, taking me outside to hear my version of the story.

"I want to leave." I said to the officer with me. "He's threatening me and broke all my plants. He has a gun, but he gave it to the neighbor over the fence. If you leave, he'll get it and shoot me. I know he will. Please, just stay while I finish getting our stuff."

"No problem, ma'am. We'll stay until you leave. Unfortunately, there is nothing we can do about the gun if it's no longer in his possession."

I quickly gathered our last bag and as I left, I felt somehow responsible for Aaron's pain.

In the days and weeks that followed I was in survival mode, my emotions heavily armored, my every thought monitored to prevent a meltdown. I had a secret that felt shredded glass cutting me to ribbons whenever I thought about it. I told no one of my rape. Shame and the fear that I got what I deserved sealed my lips.

I stayed with Isla and her husband for a few days but the house was cramped. I quickly secured a job bartending and it was there that my manager offered to help me.

"I have a spare room at my house and you can move in with the children. I know you need a place to stay."

Rick was a complete gentleman and acted as though he knew intuitively what had happened.

I moved in, and for three months Rick and I shared his house until he bought another property and moved. I rented his place and got a housemate. My longtime friend from middle school, Carmen, moved in with her toddler son and we shared the three- bedroom house. I almost felt free. Aaron would not let go, however, which was what I'd feared when I left him. The stalking began almost imme- diately.

At first, he began to park adjacent to the restaurant's parking lot where I worked and would wait for me to walk to my car at one or two in the morning. He was bold, parking where I could see him watching me. When I didn't go back to him, his tactics changed.

"Oh my God!" I screamed in the middle of the night, sucking in air as my body jerked upright. I'd been awakened from a dead sleep with my heart hammering.

There was a face peering in my bedroom window. I saw the man clearly before he slipped back into the darkness of the night. It was Aaron. I couldn't go back to sleep. I tossed and turned glancing constantly at the window afraid he'd come back. *He's watching me*, I fretted. *He'll never leave me alone.* Fear rang in my ears. *He's coming for you.*

One night I pulled into the driveway. My dashboard clock read 3:05 a.m. My lower back ached and I was tired after a busy night at work. A light mist wet my face as I stepped from the car. From the corner of my eye, I saw someone move at the side of the garage. Adrenalin surged and I hurried to the front door. With quaking hands I unlocked it and slipped inside, shutting off the porch light as I slid to the floor in tears. Frequently I felt his presence, although I could not see him. I was in constant fear that he was waiting for me, hiding in the dark.

It was Thanksgiving and we were driving to my mother's for turkey dinner. The day was dreary and outside a slow rain drizzled. I'd just reached the top of a long steady incline. I glanced in my rearview mirror at Elizabeth sleeping in her car seat. Her head fell to the side as though her neck were made of rubber. Her heart-shaped lips were parted while she snored lightly in sleep. Raine sat at the opposite end of the seat, engrossed with his transformer action figure.

We'd just begun our descent down the other side of the incline. I pressed frequently on my brake so I didn't gain too much speed. The roads were wet and slick, heavy with holiday traffic. Each time I braked, the pedal went closer to the floor. Fear pounded through my chest. I knew I was in trouble. I gripped the wheel and cut quickly right, ignoring the scream of the horn from the truck I'd cut off. I continued over, hitting gravel, pumping furiously on the brake, which now fell to the floor without springing back into place. We were heading for a giant tree. I cut the wheel hard to my left to avoid hitting it head-on. I grabbed the emergency brake yanking it upward, my foot pressed hard to the floor in vain. I squeezed my eyes shut, preparing for impact. The rear of my small car fishtailed in the loose gravel and we stopped abruptly. We'd missed the tree by inches.

Elizabeth woke with a start and let out a wail. Fear bounced around the car like a silent grenade. Raine's voice squeaked with uncertainty, "Mo-o-mmy, are we alright?"

We walked to a nearby house and called a friend who had the car towed to his garage. It was later revealed that the brake line had been neatly sliced, allowing the fluid to pump out each time I used the brake until, without fluid, the brakes failed.

Aaron was an ace mechanic.

After nearly a year of living in terror, I moved again, this time to a house protected by giant iron gates with a male roommate. In the new house, I began having *pictures* almost immediately. On our first night I put the children to bed and fell exhausted across my unmade bed. Closing my eyes, I exhaled pent up breath and enjoyed the feeling of the cool, firm mattress against my back. Suddenly the vision began.

There was a lavish party outside. Guests milled about in stylish clothing in the lower garden. A three-piece string quartet played among the scattered trees adjacent to the pool area. It was early afternoon. The day was mild with a slight breeze. Flowers were in full bloom leaving a sweet scent on the air. A man fidgeting and looking agitated approached a young couple engaged in conversation, slightly separated from the thick of the crowd.

She had dark hair and a playful light in her eye. She looked young and hopeful and her features were sharp but pretty. The man beside her was dressed differently from the others at the party, not as polished. He wore light-brown trousers held up with suspenders that looked like something a gardener or groundskeeper would wear. He had a soft cap pulled down over his forehead and was astonishingly handsome. His jaw was square and masculine. His eyes were a shade of blue that reminded me of water I'd seen only in dreams. The two were unaware of anyone else aside from each other, and I could feel their mutual attraction ripple like a current between them. As they continued to talk, the man I'd seen fidgeting moved in on the couple. His cheeks were flushed and I felt his anger and jealousy. Sweat was visible on his face and underarms as adrenaline rushed through his body.

I watched in amazement as this man raised his arm, which gripped a small handgun that I had not previously noticed. He fired the gun and the woman fell. Suddenly silence reigned as heads spun in the direction of the shot. Another shot brought down her companion. It took only seconds. Screams rang out, disrupting the party. As mayhem ensued, the uncertainty I felt at what I saw, was overwhelming.

The vision or *pictures* occurred in the first weeks of living in my new residence. I'd met my new roommate at a Mexican restaurant where I worked as a bartender. He was a regular patron. His name was Robert and he'd rented the estate from an investor friend with the promise of cleaning up the property and preparing it for resale.

The estate had been foreclosed on and fallen into disrepair. Most of the damage was from sheer neglect. Robert repaired the pool, Jacuzzi and sauna house and I had several "clean up" parties, where a dozen or so willing participants would come over to clear, clean and manicure the massive grounds. We'd fill giant yellow, dumpsters with yard debris. Because of my help, I was able to live in the house very inexpensively.

The estate was tucked securely into the hills of an auspicious California neighborhood and locked behind sturdy iron gates. It sprawled across two acres. The main house contained over three thousand square feet of opulent interior, replete with glass block and curved walls. The acreage was contained by red brick walls and had once boasted beautifully landscaped gardens that divided the space. The large pool was fenced and adjacent to a structure that housed a sauna and large Jacuzzi whose front was completely encased in glass. It was exquisite. Beyond it stood a two-story guest cottage where Robert lived. I occupied the master suite and the children shared an adjacent bedroom in the main house. I worked diligently emptying the boxes containing our possessions.

My bedroom was lavish, with a giant brick fireplace and a large walk-in closet fully lined in cedar, which seemed to beckon the awaiting piles of clothing. I longed to purchase new clothes that were worthy of such grandeur. The bathroom in my master suite sported luxurious marble floors and a sunken tub. French doors made entirely of glass led to a private garden on the lower patio. The estate won first place in the 1920s World Fair for the house most beyond its time. It was the grandest place I'd ever seen.

Elizabeth was toddling around the room as I unpacked when she pointed her fist toward the closet and whispered, "Yay, yay," her diaper swish, swish, swishing as she danced from foot to foot pointing incessantly. She continued chattering, intent on the "yay" in the closet.

Finally, I relented and leaned sideways off the bed for a clear view inside. To my surprise, I saw a young woman hiding among the clothes. I saw her for only a few seconds. She was completely oblivious to us. I leapt from my bed, and scooped up Elizabeth, and quickly shut the door leaning hard against it in astonishment.

"Holy crap," I murmured, clutching my baby. "What was that?"

The next day, I found the closet empty. Glimpses of the young woman wandering through the gardens day and night became commonplace for me. I'd glance out windows and see her on the grounds, or I'd watch as she walked across the room. a few days later I saw *pictures* of the party again. *How did everything tie together?* I wondered.

Confusion and indecision plagued me. I worried about judgment from others if I spoke about what I'd seen, so I was careful to keep quiet about the *pictures* and sightings. A couple of weeks later when I saw Robert working outside, I called to him, "Could you come up to the house later? I just want to run something by you."

"Yeah, sure. Lemme finish and take a shower."

I couldn't keep my secret any longer; I had to tell. I was nervous, but after some small talk I revealed the strange events. Robert sat quietly and listened. He fixed his hooded gray eyes on the wall behind me. When I finished my story he spoke in a voice so quiet I had to strain to listen.

"I see her too. She comes to me in my dreams." He shifted his gaze to me, stroked his beard, and continued.

"Sometimes," he said, "I dream I'm in the Jacuzzi and she comes and asks for my help. She pleads for protection." He finished and raised his eyebrows in an "I'm crazy too" kind of way.

Robert was ten years my senior and had never spoken to me of anything metaphysical. I was shocked and excited to hear his reply. Robert continued, "It wasn't long after we moved in that I started having dreams about her. Sometimes I'm in different places around the house or grounds in my dreams, but she always comes. I started to think maybe I've been drinking too much or something," he said rolling ice cubes through the silky scotch in his tumbler.

We talked for a couple of hours, making comparisons and feeling relief that we both saw her, although differently. Afterward, Robert did some research on the background of the property. It was easy to find an old article relating to the murders. The incident was exactly what I had seen in the *pictures* and had occurred years earlier. While Robert dug into information about the estate, I decided to call Boots, the psychic my mother had taken us to years before, for advice on what to do.

"Well," she said, "as I listen to you talk, it feels like the woman does not understand that she is dead. She may be looking for a safe place to hide and trying to find her family members."

"Really? You think she doesn't know she's dead?" I asked.

"Yes, it can happen when there is sudden or tragic death. There can be an inability to transition to "the other side.""

"The other side? You mean like heaven?" "Yes, something like heaven.""

"What can I do?" I asked.

"Surround her in white light, pray and ask for angelic help to assist her in her transition."

Confused, I asked "What do you mean?" "Do you believe in angels?"

"Yes, totally," I said, thinking of Maggie. "Do you know how to meditate?"

"Yes, you taught me when I was fourteen, I still do it sometimes."

"In the same way you meditate, bring her into your mind's eye and see her surrounded in white light. While doing this, pray and ask the angels to come and help her to transition to the other side. Encourage her to go toward the light, to go with the angels. That should work. If you have trouble, call me back but I feel you can do it. And I'm picking up that you need to ground your energy; it's all over the place," she finished.

I began to pray and meditate. I asked the angels to come and assist the woman in her transition. *She's lost and scared and she doesn't know she's dead. Please come help her.* Twice I'd spent about a half an hour in meditation before anything aside from relaxation occurred. On my third attempt I was successful. After breakfast, I sat in the kitchen on a built-in banquet against a large bay window where morning sunlight fell across my shoulders in soothing warmth. The experience was remarkable. I'm uncertain how much time passed while I prayed and meditated. Suddenly, I saw the woman in my mind's eye. I felt her confusion and fear. I sent her telepathic messages. *Don't be afraid. You're not alone. The angels have been looking for you. They're waiting for you. Look for the light.* I felt her acknowledgment and relief. I repeated my message again and again.

Without warning I saw a bright light. The light had an exceptionally high vibration and sounded like music without a tune. I knew the loving presence was an angel. Tears fell in a constant stream from beneath my closed eyes but I could not feel the rest of my body as I watched the event unfold. The bodies of energy that were the woman and angel's merged and evolved, disappearing from my consciousness.

My body was covered in goose flesh and tears flowed freely. It was the most extraordinary thing to witness and be part of, and it left a stunning impression I have never forgotten.

I no longer saw her and Robert had no more dreams of the lost and lonely woman. I learned to trust myself a little more when the *pictures* came. I had other *pictures* while living at the estate. These seemed to increase in frequency and for the first time I saw *pictures* that occurred in real time instead of past or future events. During this part of my life I acknowledged the frequent visits from the *light-body* and had begun talking to it in my mind and out loud. I still felt foolish and I kept the information to myself, but an opening into the possibility that I wasn't crazy had begun.

Eventually, the estate was ready for resale and I had to move again. I rented a small three-bedroom house with no roommates, just the kids and me.

One night, as I sat at the top of my bed and leaned against the cool wall preparing to meditate, I felt the presence of the *light- body* and I asked in my mind, "*Who are you?*"

It responded, "*I am you, I am your guide.*"

"*Okay, what does that mean?*" I asked.

"*It means I am part of you and here always to help you, to guide you along your way. I am what you need most.*"

"*Are you the one that has always been there? The one I have always seen?*" I asked.

"*Yes*" came the reply.

"*Will you always be here?*" I questioned.

"*Yes, I am part of you.*" "*What's your name?*"

"*You may call me anything you wish.*"

"*Can I call you my father guide?*" I asked, because the energy felt fatherly, protective, and loving. Something my father was unable to give.

"Yes," the light-body answered.

"Okay because I never had a father," I replied.

Silence followed and I heard nothing more so I opened my eyes. I continued to have a dialogue almost nightly with my guide and the feeling of loneliness began to wane. I also understood that the *voice* I heard was just another way my intuition manifested, like the *knowing*. But I was still learning how it all tied together.

I did my best to comprehend the information I received. Yet despite my new understanding and despite the fact that two years had passed since I'd left Aaron, I was still afraid. I was leery that he was around every corner.

THE SWEETHEART RAPIST AND HIS CASTLE

The tiny house sat alone near a jetty, surrounded by sand and trees. The man liked it here, away from prying eyes. He needed a private place to entertain. Having a family had been disappointing, only adding to his anger and frustration. Now, though, he had a place of his own, secluded and quiet. He smiled and whistled a tune as his anticipation surged. He was excited to have a weekend guest in his new place. It felt good. He checked to make sure things were perfect one more time before he left to pick up his visitor.

A large roll of tape next to the handy blindfold he'd made himself, sat on the bedside table. A new tube of lubricant, smooth and clean was there too. He reached for the small mirror that came with a shiny metal straw and snorted the last of the cocaine on the smudged surface, enjoying the burn. He rubbed what was left of the bitter powder across his gums. Satisfied, he grabbed his mask on the way out; this one had bright green eyes, which suited him fine.

The young girl felt a thrill in the deepest part of her belly. She was camping with the boy who made her heart pound—the boy she was in love with. Her brother and his friend had come along too, but were at the next campsite so the young lovers could be alone. A permanent smile lit up her pretty face.

They lay together under the stars in their tent breathing hard and making out. The girl was fifteen now and had everything she could want. Her glossy, black hair lay in provocative curls against her exposed chest, accentuating the white lace of her bra. They laughed as they passed a joint back and forth and planned their weekend.

"Let's hike and lie naked on the lake tomorrow," she said with a mischievous smile.

"Anything you want, baby," he said, exhaling smoke as he reached for her. The sound of feet over loose rocks surprised them.

"Hey, what's that? Shush, be quiet. Shit, is that a flashlight?" she asked, alarm rising in her voice.

"You two better get out here," came a voice from outside the tent. "I have a gun and I'm not fucking around."

The scared young couple did as they were told.

"What the fuck?" the young man said as he lifted the tent's flap and stepped out.

The man stood just outside of the tent with his arm extended, pointing his gun at the young man's face. "Shut the fuck up, buddy and get over to the car before I blow your head off."

The young man balled his hands into fists and stood his ground. The man grabbed the girl's hair at the back of her head and pressed the snout of the gun against the soft tissue of her temple.

"I mean it, motherfucker."

The masked man forced the boy into the trunk of his car. He took the girl, crying and stumbling, to his truck parked nearby and placed her face down across the seat, covering her face with the mask he'd worn.

"Stay down. Don't make me shoot you."

Hearing commotion, the girl's brother hurried to his sister's tent.

"Hey, what's going on?" he asked as he peeled back the tent flap, finding it empty. He turned toward a loud bang and saw the trunk of a car fly open. He watched in surprise as his sister's boyfriend sprang out clutching a tire iron and screaming.

"He has her! He took your sister!"

The man with the mask started his truck and backed out quickly. He jammed the truck into drive prematurely making the gears grind, just as the two boys ran toward him.

"You better stop! Hey!"

A tire iron smashed into the truck's passenger window, nearly shattering the glass completely. The man, angry and shaking with adrenalin, fired two shots through his rear window as he pressed harder on the accelerator.

The girl was crying and pleading with her abductor. "Pleease let me g-go, please. I won't tell, I promise. Oh, God, please. Don't hurt me," she begged.

10

The helicopter hovered like a hawk eyeing its prey, its giant blades whooped in an excited rhythm. Police cars from all directions screeched to a halt, effectively sealing off the building. There would be no entry or exit. Car doors swung wide, releasing eager dogs that pulled against leather harnesses.

A local auto body shop filled the television screen. A handcuffed man, flanked by officers sporting grim expressions, kept his head bowed and shuffled toward the camera.

"That's all for now. Stay with News Channel 3 for updates on this developing story." The camera panned back to the newscaster behind his desk, his eyes alive with the excitement of a breaking story.

"Okay, Terry, thanks again and stay with us at News Channel 3 as we bring you the latest developments in this story."

In the corner of the screen the man in handcuffs glanced up into the camera's lenses. His chilling stare looked directly into my eyes. I was astounded, frozen with disbelief. My stomach twisted as though zapped by an electric current. Panic roared through me. I spun around and hurried to the kitchen. I searched the phonebook for a number and mindlessly dialed.

"I know the man they're arresting right now, the one on TV. Can you tell me what he is being charged with?" I said into the phone,

"I'm sorry, ma'am, I'm afraid we can't release that information. Who did you say you are and what is your connection to the man?"

"I need to speak with whoever's in charge. Please, it's important. Please." My body felt like a thousand pounds of cement. I sank to the floor. My scalp tightened with the prickling sensation of dread.

After an eternity on hold, a man answered the phone, "Dade County D. A., this is Markus Short."

He was soft spoken but rigid. He refused to tell me anything until I explained who I was. I told him everything. I told him with shame that burned my lips what I'd told no one; I confessed my connection and all that it meant. When I finished neither of us spoke. Finally, he said, "He's being charged with rape."

My stomach plunged and I felt the truth wash over me like stinging needles.

"He is suspected of multiple assaults, serial rape. The media have dubbed him the 'The Sweetheart Rapist' and we've been looking for him for several years. After what you've told me, I'll need to send someone to your home immediately," he continued. "We will need to interview you. We will need you to testify."

I was astonished because I'd never even heard of the crimes. I didn't read the papers or watch the news. I was grossly uninformed. Suddenly, there was a humming in my ears and my hand shook as I hung up the phone. I stared at the wall, my mind as empty as a hollowed tree. I stumbled to the bathroom and vomited until there was nothing left. I panted on my knees and clutched the cold porcelain bowl as the *pictures* of the man in the mask came racing back. They rose up fierce and suffocating, and forced my body into a cold sweat.

Oh my god, oh my god, this is my fault. I should have known. I did know, didn't I? I saw him, Did I know somewhere within myself who it was and what he was doing? Oh God, forgive me. What have I done? I believed that somehow I had the power to alter the events. If only I'd been able to

*face what I thought, I should have known. I sank into a dark tunnel where
the only sound was the roaring in my ears.*

The story was covered on nearly every television station in the
area and the newspaper ran an article the next day. I carefully cut it
out and hid it.

Recent Assaults May Have Broken Two-year Rape Case.

Sheriff's investigators hunted two years for the East County "The
Sweetheart Rapist," even setting up decoy officers in amorous
settings in an attempt to trap him. Efforts to find a suspect proved
unproductive until this week when a 31-year-old man was arrested
for the kidnap and rape of a 15-year-old girl and a 17-year-old
teenager. The string of sexual assaults occurred primarily during
warm weather in secluded areas of East County frequented by
lovers. There were seven assaults within the sheriff's jurisdiction and
two inside local city limits. Captain Raymond Nulty said Tuesday
that after last week's incident in which a 15-year-old girl camping on
Richmond's levee was kidnapped and raped, crucial information
identifying a suspect came into the investigation division...

My fingertips were numb as I held the paper and finished the article. I hadn't slept since the discovery of the rapist. I felt like a guilty
co-conspirator-- shameful and dirty. *Three-year-old rape case? That's
before I left him. When people find out who I am,* I thought, *they will think
I'm dirty too and what will happen to my children?* I imagined the
kindergarten mothers whispering, fingers pointed at my innocent
Raine. "He's the child of a rapist," they'd say. "Keep your children
away from him." *How can I protect them? How will I tell my children,
that their father is a serial rapist and their mother should have known
all along?*

Self-blame festered and infected me. Past events looped endlessly
in my mind and I chided myself for not putting the pieces together
before. Not only had I seen the *pictures* of the man in the mask, but
there had been many other things I'd rejected and disregarded in
the past.

I'd felt someone watching me the night I talked to Honey on the phone and I *knew,* both intuitively and consciously, it was Aaron hiding somewhere in the dark. I'd had a flash in my mind's eye of Aaron lying in the dirt. It had happened more than once and I'd told myself, *He'll trust me more when he sees I am honest. If he's willing to watch me, he must really love me. He doesn't want to get hurt.* I couldn't acknowledge the disturbing truth.

I'd come home late one night when I was pregnant with Elizabeth and Aaron was sitting in the dark. I felt disturbing energy from him, like he was reliving something. I saw it literally glow like a ghostly light around him. I'd been so scared that I found myself holding my breath multiple times for the next several days. I was certain he had done something horrible. I *knew* it. I physically kept my distance from him because I didn't want to *know* what it was he had done. If I got too close, if he touched me, I risked the *knowing.*

How many times had Bernadette, Aaron's mother, told the story of losing her lung and her friend at the hand of her murdering husband? "That was the most horrible day of my life." She'd say. "That man ain't no better'n a dog. Leavin' three little boys with that legacy. What a gift, huh?"

And over and over she recounted the story of Aaron's accident and how *she* had suffered saying, "I was just sick with worry that my boy would die. There was so many expenses, you know? I could hardly keep up and thank God for that money cause raisin 'them boys with no help was no picnic neither."

I knew Aaron hated and blamed her for keeping his money. He said so on many occasions calling her a "selfish bitch."

Just a couple of months after I'd left him-- after my rape-- he'd shown up at the house I was renting with Carmen. I was home alone and surprised when I opened the door.

"What? You don't think I know where you live?" he'd asked, pushing his way through the door.

"What do you want, Aaron?" I responded.

"I want to know where my kids are living," he said looking around my living room.

"Well now you know so I guess that's it. You can go now." My insides were trembling. I hated that he had that effect on me.

"I want you to leave us alone Aaron. Please," I said.

"Maybe I will, but you'll have to do something for me. Give me a blow job one last time," he said.

"You are a disgusting pig. Just get out!" I screamed.

"I'll leave you alone, I promise. I won't bother you. You owe it to me. Just do it quick," he said unbuckling his belt.

I don't know how I got there, but I found myself on my knees, crying while Aaron twisted my hair in his fist and pushed himself into my mouth. The shame I felt after what I'd done was bigger and deeper than any other event in my life. It cemented my feelings of powerlessness and self-hate.

And finally, when he'd come home casually talking and laughing about the woman on the freeway he'd frightened simply because she'd cut him off, I knew he was sick and needed help. I saw that something had shifted; he wasn't rational. I saw it but I did nothing. Living with him required me to be dead inside, to bury my feelings. That was how I survived.

There'd been times in the past when he touched me, his warm fingers brushing my skin and I thought I felt the energy of other women. I thought I felt their fear and revulsion. Their essence was attached to his skin and when he touched me it crawled like a virus, infecting me. But I told myself it was absurd, impossible. I blocked the experiences and the *knowing* from my conscious mind. I lived in a constant state of fear and dread.

Now as the days passed, I combed my memory trying to dig up the things I had hidden. I became obsessed.

At the same time that I reflected on the past, I had to grasp the realities of the day before, when a female detective and her partner knocked on my door. They stood rigid on my porch, wearing crisp uniforms and serious expressions. I invited them in and we sat in my kitchen at a small round table, a recording device placed on its center. After stating the date, time and place the sheriff looked at me with compassion. I had not expected and could not accept it. *She doesn't know it's my fault too.*

"We have a pile of evidence—some circumstantial, some physical. The physical evidence is in the lab being tested now," the brown-eyed sheriff told me. "And we think you may be the link that can tie much of the circumstantial evidence together. I need to ask you some questions about the mask you mentioned in your conversation with Mr. Short. Can you describe for me the masks you made for your son?" she asked in a soft voice.

"Yes," I replied. My body was ice cold and buzzed as if I were plugged into the wall.

"I bought beanies. You know, the black ones you wear for skiing? It was actually his idea to make super hero masks."

"Yes," the sheriff said, "go on." She pushed the recorder toward me.

"At first, I just cut the holes for the eyes, but later I started sewing around the cutouts with brightly colored thread to make a Spiderman mask."

"A Spiderman mask for your son, you mean?"

"Yes," I replied, and locked my eyes with hers to steady myself. "And can you tell me what colors you used?" she asked.

"Well," I said as I licked my dry lips. "All kinds of colors. Green, pink, yellow and orange. Bright colors like the real Spiderman." I swallowed the acid that rose at the back of my throat.

"Can you tell me why you made so many masks?"

My underarms were now in a full sweat, unaffected by the carefully applied layers of deodorant. I clasped my hands tightly to stop the shaking.

"Well," I hesitated. "They kept disappearing so I just made new ones. I thought Raine lost them or hid them."

"And can you tell me, did you ever find the missing masks?"

"No, I didn't."

Although it would never be proven, I *knew* some of the masks I'd made with love for my son were used to debase and terrify women.

I listened to the frightening detail of the rapes. I was horrified when I discovered how long the attacks had been occurring, and I *knew* there were more that had not been discovered. The sheriff's detective laid out the circumstantial evidence that my testimony could validate.

I could confirm the time frames of the assaults and the cars that Aaron had access to. Sometimes he brought vehicles home while he worked on them, vehicles that were spotted at the crime scenes. I could also speak to Aaron's familiarity with certain remote areas, and weeks later I would accompany an officer to a house we'd rented in a secluded area, grossly close to two of the rapes.

I realized as the sheriff spoke that the house and one of the rapes she referred to had happened on the same night that I'd found Aaron sitting alone in the dark, but I couldn't speak it out loud. *My fault*, I thought, *my fault*.

There were more questions about the masks I'd made for my son and about whether I had cheated on Aaron. And i f so, where and when it had occurred. It turned out, that Aaron had spoken of the infidelity to several of his victims.

I discovered that all but one of his victims had blonde hair like me. They were told this was the reason they had been chosen. Aaron would degrade the women saying, "My girlfriend was a real blonde, I'm disappointed you're not." The sickening connections went on and on. There were nine victims in the state's case, but they suspected Aaron of many more rapes and assaults that they couldn't prove, dating back for years.

As the sheriff talked my mind regressed to some five-and-a- half years before when I was sixteen and pregnant with Raine. A police car had pulled up in front of our house and two officers stepped out on the lawn.

"Good afternoon, ma'am. Is Aaron Goddard here?" one of the officers asked.

"No. Why?" I asked.

"Does he drive a tow truck?" the officer responded. He sported slick mirrored sunglasses.

"Yes, he's at work right now." "What time will he be home?"

I shrugged my shoulders, sizing up the situation. "Was he home last night?" the officer continued.

"Yes he was. I don't think he got called out," I answered quickly, knowing he had been gone most of the night. My defense of Aaron was automatic. It's what I did. "What's this about?" I'd asked as my anxiety grew.

"We're investigating a rape that happened last night in the area where a tow truck was spotted," the officer said watching me.

"That's ridiculous," I replied. "Aaron would never hurt anyone and he was home last night."

I believed Aaron couldn't rape or hurt another person. I remembered thinking the police were wasting their time. We'd just moved in together and I was completely naïve. Now, as I remembered the incident and my lie I felt arrogant, foolish and responsible. But again, I didn't tell the sheriff.

"He'll be arraigned tomorrow," she continued, "but the preliminary hearing hasn't been set. We will notify you when it is. In the meantime, the D.A. will schedule an appointment with you to go over your testimony and discuss what you can expect going forward."

"I have conditions as to what I will testify to," I said gazing across the room at the scattered toys on the floor. Isla had Elizabeth and Raine so I could have privacy.

"I want to talk with the prosecutor. There have to be conditions or I can't help."

I met with the assistant D.A. later that week. I didn't want to testify about my own rape and the prosecutor agreed saying, "When he was arrested, he asked the officer, 'Is this about what I did to Nita?' We didn't know who Nita was or what he was talking about. Now we do. It's too messy to include your rape. You're considered Aaron's 'common law wife' and the rape will muddy the water. I think your testimony will substantiate much of circumstantial evidence we have and it's extremely valuable to the case."

As the prosecutor talked, I thought about Aaron's past and the trunk that his hateful father locked him in. Now, years later, Aaron was locking other men in trunks. I would later share the information with a court appointed psychiatrist and recount Aaron's history with his mother Bernadette.

The prosecutor continued to recite the ways my testimony could link Aaron to his crimes, covering the information we would and wouldn't use. Without my testimony there would be a number of holes in the prosecution's case. He agreed to protect my children from the media by not releasing their names. Protecting them was all that mattered to me.

I suspected there was something intrinsically wrong with me, because I'd trusted and loved Aaron deeply. *How could I have been fooled? How could anyone love such a man?* I was ashamed to admit that truth to anyone. I wanted to believe Aaron was innocent and incapable of such heinous crimes. I secretly held on to that hope for years even though I *knew* the truth. *One day they'll find the real rapist and it will have been a bad dream.*

I had no one I could confide in and my mother and sisters wanted nothing to do with the situation, so I faced the drama alone. No one wanted to be affiliated with a dirty, disgusting rapist and his family. My own family judged me. I had brought shame to them by my involvement with Aaron, who was now, front-page news. They had warned me all along.

The preliminary hearing was held weeks later. I sat alone in a tiny room, jittery. My foot bounced uncontrollably and I bit my nails until they bled, as I waited to be called to testify at the closed hearing. The idea that I had to look directly at Aaron terrified me, still.

The purpose of a preliminary hearing was to establish whether the state had enough evidence to hold Aaron in custody for a trial. The state presented evidence and his victims gave brief testimonies. We were sequestered separately and I had no idea who else was involved.

I learned that day that Aaron's prosecution, if successful, would set a new precedent for how rape cases were charged. In the past, a rape charge carried a seven-year sentence. But Aaron would be charged for each violation separately. Instead of a rape charge per assault, each rape would be broken down into acts which would each carry a separate sentence. For instance, one rape might include use of a deadly weapon, oral copulation, sodomy, false imprisonment, kidnapping, forcible rape and so on. Aaron was ordered to stand trial. The Judge raised his bail from $200,000 to $500,000 ensuring he would be in custody until his trial. The article in the paper the next day read in part:

The Sweetheart Rapist Suspect Ordered To Stand Trial

A municipal court judge ordered the accused "Sweet Heart Rapist," Aaron Goddard, to stand trial on 55 felonies Thursday, and praised the rape victims who testified for their strength of character and courage.

After a closed preliminary hearing a municipal court judge ruled, "There is enough evidence to try Goddard on 10 counts of forcible rape, 21 counts of other forcible sex acts, nine counts of kidnapping, 14 counts of false imprisonment and one count of endangering a child." The Superior Court Judge said, "Each of the eight young women who have testified as a victim of these crimes has demonstrated the power and resilience of the human spirit and has done that in a way that has humbled and inspired the listeners."

After giving my testimony at the preliminary hearing, I began to receive death threats by phone. They were completely unexpected and I'd falsely assumed I was safe with Aaron in jail.

"Hello," I said

"You want to die, bitch?" came the shocking reply of a man's voice.

"Who is this?"

"If you testify, you will die. Think about it, bitch." And the line went dead.

Other calls included bomb threats. "Bombs are easy to hide in a car. Kaboom! You'll never even know it." Each threat paralyzed me with fear.

The calls were constant. They came day and night. The prosecutor's office set up phone recording devices with tracers on my phones. I received calls while at work, threatening bombs in the wheel wells of my car so that I had to notify police to check my vehicle each time before I left. I'd stand in the parking lot after midnight, exhausted and in disbelief as sniffer dogs checked my vehicle. The people responsible for the terrorizing threats were never caught and I was suffocating in fear. I had bodyguards and escorts to and from work arranged by a close friend who was active military.

Raine, just five-years-old, sat quietly beside me in the car while men with guns sat in the front seat. They entered our house while we waited in the car and Raine asked, "Mommy why does the man have a gun?"

"Because they're keeping us safe. It's okay, baby, don't worry."

When it was time for the trial, I testified despite my fear and despite the death threats. The victims and witnesses in the case weren't allowed in the courtroom, either before or after our testimony.

The day of trial, we sat sequestered in an airless room, waiting to be called to the stand. It was the first time I' d seen his victims and I was overcome with guilt and worry. I fretted that they would discover that I'd loved him and borne his children. That they would blame me as I blamed myself. I didn't realize that they already knew who I was.

No one spoke in a room filled with trepidation. Each woman sat engrossed in her own world of pain and anxiety. I kept my head down and eyes averted. The door opened and a bailiff called a name. A young woman stood, I glanced up at the same moment and our eyes met. I recognized her from a pre-law class I'd attended at a local community college months before. She'd sat just two rows in front of me. I'd noticed her because of her blonde hair and striking features. She was pretty.

"I remember you from class," she said. "I'm going to get that son-of-a-bitch for you and your kids."

Her statement and fierce determination floored me. I was astonished that she knew who I was and didn't hate or blame me. Her words were unbelievable and emotion welled in my throat.

I couldn't respond. I burned with guilt. I longed to have the grace and courage that she possessed. *How can she defend me*? I thought. She saved me that day from crushing self-judgment. She opened a door that suggested I was his victim too. I'd never considered such a thing.

Following my testimony, I left in a daze. After a three-week trial, Aaron was found guilty. Prior to sentencing, I methodically packed our belongings. I'd decided to move away.

I knew we had to move very far away when this ordeal was finished, but I didn't know where to go. As it turned out, the answer was delivered to me.

I joined Carmen and Cecily, girlfriends I'd known since middle school, on a vacation to Hawaii for a week. It felt like the perfect time to get away from the immense stress that Aaron's arrest had brought. My mother agreed to keep the children. The three of us lay together on the beach one day, reading books and tanning, when I heard bagpipes being played.

"Hey," I said sitting up searching the beach for the piper. "Do you guys hear that?"

"What?" Cecily asked.

"Bagpipes. I know I heard them." "Nope," came they replied in unison.

Hours later, we met two young men from Scotland, Ian and Keith, who were on a year-long world tour together. I *knew* Scotland was where I needed to go. Through Ian, I contacted his family and rented a flat that would become available a couple of months later. After the trial and sentencing, I sold everything we owned, bought three one-way tickets and planned our move.

Two weeks before left, I stood packing boxes, sorting what to take with us. It was a bright afternoon and Raine, seven-years-old now, played in the back yard with his friend Tommy. Elizabeth, age four, had just joined the boys for snacks under the cool shade of a tree. Their voices floated through an open window.

"I don't like bologna," Elizabeth whined. "Here," Raine said. "Take the peanut butter."

"Ooh, can I have the grape juice?" Tommy asked.

Our house was located on a busy corner. I watched as a small red car pulled to the curb. I watched through the window next to my front door. The hair raised along my arms. Dread coiled in my stomach like a snake. Two men got out and one reached into the back seat. The *knowing* told me they meant harm. Simultaneously, several things happened. My skin went tight, my mouth dry, and panic pounded through my body. It felt like I was in a dream. I yelled into the backyard, "Raine, Raine!"

He turned toward my voice, his baby-fine hair lifting with the breeze. "What, Mom?"

"Get Elizabeth and you and Tommy come in this instant!" My voice was urgent. "Hurry, Raine, right now!"

"Okay, okay, Mommy, but what's a matter?" he asked clearly frightened, scrambling from under the tree.

"Go to your room," I said holding the screen door open. "Get down on your hands and knees! Crawl down the hall and get under the bed and hide! Don't come out until I tell you to. Go!"

He did as he was told, crawling down the hall and pushing Elizabeth's rear-end in front of him.

I screamed, "Shut the door and don't come out until I say!"

I raced to the phone and dialed the police. I watched as the men split up, one headed to the side of the house towards the backyard gate clutching a handgun, the other held a rifle and came to the front door. My blood felt like syrup. I could feel my heartbeat in my lips.

"Police emergency," a woman said.

"I need help," I gasped. "There are men here with guns and they're going to kill us." *I sound crazy*, I thought as I spoke. "I testified against Aaron Goddard!" I cried.

"Who?"

"The Sweetheart Rapist. I testified and they're going to kill me. Please, my children are here," I croaked as I began to cry.

"Stay calm, ma'am. We're on the way. I'm going to stay on the phone with you, okay?"

I told the operator my address. The next moments were a blur. My head pounded and my entire body shook. Everything moved in slow motion and at high speed all at once.

The man with the rifle was on the porch. He cupped his hand on the glass and looked inside. Our eyes met. Dark unwashed hair lay in waves around his face. A scar ran across his cheek. His glassy eyes held my gaze and he raised his weapon taking aim. I couldn't think. I was completely immobile. I lost the feeling in my legs. I clutched the phone's receiver to my ear. I was aware that the dispatcher was talking and I heard myself grunt in response.

Sirens wailed in the distance. I waited to feel gunshots pierce my skin. Seconds ticked by, instead of shooting the man put two fingers in his mouth and whistled. Tires screeched as they pulled away onto the busy street. Seconds later, several police cars came from the opposite direction, sirens blaring and lights ablaze.

When the men were gone, I dropped the phone and ran on rubber legs to the bedroom. Police and barking dogs surrounded our house. Dropping to my knees, I peered under the bed, where three very frightened children lay, just as instructed.

In the distance, I heard the front door open. "We're safe!" I shouted. "We're back here!"

"You are such a trooper, Raine, such a good boy. You did good," I cooed.

In the voice of a terrified little boy, he asked, "What's wrong, Mommy? Is everything alright?"

Tears welled up in both of our eyes and I said, "Yes, Raine, everything is fine. Mommy was having a fire drill and you were so brave. You are such a good listener. Come on out now."

I wiped the tears from my face and reached under the bed, pulling a wide-eyed, Elizabeth by her arms across the hardwood floor into my lap, with Raine only seconds behind. I held them both in a tight embrace. Poor Tommy had not uttered a word.

Raine rode his bike down the street to Tommy's and I held Elizabeth on my hip as I talked with police officers.

"It's not safe for you here, ma'am. Do you have somewhere to go?"

"Yes, I do. My friends are on the way here now. I will go somewhere where no one can find us."

"Will you need an escort? We'd be happy to follow you."

"No, thank you. God, I just can't believe this. How could he know I was leaving when he's in jail? Is this about my leaving the country or is he still trying to kill me?"

"I wish I could help, ma'am. There will be an investigation and D.A. Short will be notified."

Several weeks passed between Aaron's conviction and his sentencing hearing. He had been convicted of 49 felonies. Six of the counts were subject to mistrial. The news headlines read:

Sweetheart Rapist Gets 142 Years.

The "The Sweetheart Rapist" of East County was sentenced yesterday to 142 years and four months in prison. The sentence, imposed during a dramatic hearing by a judge who said the evidence was the most devastating he had seen in years on the bench, ended what the prosecutor called "probably the most serious sexual assault case in the history of the county." As outlined by prosecutors, the assaults followed a pattern; they involved women parked in remote areas, usually with male companions. A man, often wearing a ski mask and carrying a gun and flashlight, would force the man into the trunk of the car, then drive the women to another location and sexually assault her. The victims ranged in age from 15 to 33 years. Six of the victims were teenagers.

I'd given notice at work the week before the men came to my house. Many of my friends exclaimed, "Are you crazy? You can't move to a foreign country where you don't know a soul and have no job and no one to help you."

"Yes I can," I'd replied. "I know it's what I'm supposed to do next. It will all work out" and I *knew* it would. I wasn't afraid. I began saving money immediately for our tickets, but in truth, I didn't have a lot of cushion. I knew I had to find work right away. And I *knew* I would.

In the weeks prior to our departures, I stayed with my children at a secret location to keep them safe. We were running for our lives. During and after the trial, I became paranoid--unable to sleep, afraid of the slightest noise or shadow. I could no longer sleep with the closet door closed, afraid someone was lurking inside. I was terrified to enter a darkened room, afraid of who might be hiding there. I obsessively checked the rearview mirrors while driving, sure that I was being followed. I had recurring nightmares that Aaron was after me and I couldn't find a place to hide. I woke up panting or screaming. I was unable to get into a car without getting on my hands and knees first and checking beneath it for bombs. I trusted no one.

11

————

The cold splintered my bones as it burrowed into my body through the stone bench where I sat, shivering in the sun. I was on the Isle of Skye, touring Dunvegan Castle in Scotland. I gazed at the massive gardens from my perch. The surroundings spurred a memory of a past life—a memory I'd never had before. The *pictures* started immediately and revealed pieces of an incarnation I hadn't known existed.

I saw a man with bright blue eyes and a wild beard, whose kindness and love for his daughter could not be hidden. I *knew* I had been his daughter in that life, and the visions were a memory of my soul's experience. I *knew* too, that they had visited this castle and had been going there since the girl's childhood -- my childhood.

In the first vision, the bearded man was outside on the castle grounds enjoying a warm day. He laughed and I felt his gentleness and the pain he still carried from the loss of his wife, who had died when the girl was a young child. He had a quick mind and a volatile temper, but he was devoted to his daughter in a manner that was unusual for a man of his time.

In the next *picture* the girl, who was about fifteen-years-old, stood at the back gate of Dunvegan, squinting against the sun. She watched and prayed for a ship to enter the loch and deliver the man she loved, a Spaniard whom she'd met the summer before. Dampness weighted her skirts and bitter cold burned her feet. But she was unaware of any discomfort. I *knew* the ship would not arrive and that the girl would never see the man again.

Next, I saw a fierce battle outside of the castle. The girl's father had been caught unaware and forced to fight a war between clans that were not his.

In the *pictures*, I watched as her father died at the end of another man's sword. Human filth, rage and bloody soil left a reek of death in the air. The girl was taken to a dark and cold windowless chamber where she, along with other inhabitants of the castle, waited for days until the danger passed.

In that life, I *knew* the girl wouldn't recover from both the loss of her father and her lover. Death would find her before she bore children or felt the arms of a man she longed for – she would die in youth of a broken and lonely heart.

The *knowing* was so powerful and the *pictures* so clear no matter how foolish they sounded I *knew* the truth and through the experience, I became more grounded in my gifts.

As I walked through the impressive castle that day, I *knew* what lay behind the walls of rooms that I couldn't see. In my mind's eye was a narrow staircase, off of a room that was now painted dark blue. A room not visible to our group. When I asked the tour guide about it he said, "Oh, are you a friend of the family then?"

"No," I'd replied, "but I've seen it before."

He eyed me suspiciously.

Since then, I've had dozens of similar experiences with the *visions* and the *knowing*, though that was my only past-life memory. Others involved my ability to connect with energies that most couldn't see, such as the old woman I'd seen in my friend's house as a child. She wasn't actually there but her energetic imprint was. I drew an inner strength from each episode growing more confident and secure. This was the gift that Scotland gave me.

The knowledge that my abilities delivered allowed me to understand and piece together the events of my life . This understanding released the need for judgment, and the letting go of judgment made room for forgiveness, which in turn gave birth to self-awareness. I began to trust my intuition and take responsibility for my life. I no longer felt the need to place blame or label my choices or myself as "bad."

When I'd fled from the United States, I hadn't known what to expect in Scotland. I arrived at a bustling Heathrow airport in London with two exhausted children and a mountain of luggage.

After going through customs, we boarded another flight to Edinburgh where we were greeted by the brother of the man who I'd met in Hawaii, whose furnished flat I'd rented before leaving the States.

The man's name was Regan and he recognized us immediately, although he'd never seen us. His face lit up with happiness, as though we were old friends and he waved and shouted, "Nita, Nita! This wey."

As we moved toward him he gathered me in a firm embrace. "Oh, it's good ti see ye. How wes your trip?" he asked in a thick Scottish brogue.

"It was long, but the children are great travelers," I said looking at Raine who gripped Elizabeth's hand tightly. "We are tired, though."

"I cen well imagine. Let me get ye to the flat then. I have some fruit and other bits and pieces there fur yi if yir hungry."

"Oh my gosh, Regan, thank you."

Raine pulled at my sleeve, "I need the bathroom," he said.

"Oh," Regan answered. "The toilet is just there," he said pointing. "Come on then, I'll take yi."

Raine glared at him suspiciously.

"It's alright, Raine. You go with Regan and I'll take Elizabeth." "

To the baaaath-roooom," Raine said as he opened his mouth wide, exaggerating the word for Regan, "Not the toilet."

Regan was warm and friendly and took us directly to our flat, which we were renting from him. As promised, a large basket filled with fruit, biscuits, jam, and cheese sat on the counter of the small kitchen.

"Well then," Ian said after unloading us. "I'll leave yi to it then. I've written my phone code for yi should you need anythin and there is information for the markets and bus schedules an that, into the city. I'll check in after a day or so. Right, cheers then," he finished and hugged me goodbye.

"Thank you so much, Regan, the place is really nice."

The flat was located just outside of Edinburgh and days after our arrival, I took short bus rides into the city and things seemed to fall into place.

My nostril's flared as I tipped them toward the sky, breathing in the aroma of yeast and hops so prevalent in the city of Edinburgh. Cold mist moistened my cheeks in the early morning, despite the late summer month, as I made my way down Princess Street, known as the Royal Mile. Fragments of conversation floated past.

"Oh aye, hen. I ken whet ye meen. Those wee barins Ill ge up ti no good, so they will."

The two women chatted happily as they walked. Behind them a couple strolled arm in arm. "Aye, aye yer right, luv," the man said, "You've ti listen if ye"... Another man clutching a briefcase hurried by gently bumping against me and mumbling, "Pardon, luv, cheers-ta."

I took it all in. Although I was a visitor, I felt at home.

Edinburgh Castle loomed over the city, like a giant sentry standing guard. Its origin dated as far back as the ninth century B.C., but its first royal occupation was by King David I during the twelfth century. The medieval castle was constructed by determined Scotsmen, who would be proud to witness that their blood they had put into the medieval design still lived on some 800 years later. I admired the ancient stone structures that dotted the landscape, sculpted with steep turrets, stained and blackened with streaks from acid rain.

I was delighted to find that on Sunday mornings, bagpipers lined Princess Street, playing their Chanter and Drone for passersby. At the sweet rendition of Amazing Grace I cried, my heart was filled with the pipes' wail and my soul was delivered home. The lyrical speech of the Scottish people sounded oddly familiar and had a calming effect on me. I had no difficulty understanding their thick brogues and in no time my children and I sounded as though we were born there. I couldn't recall ever feeling so at peace.

I walked the city streets in search of a job, and on my third day, I found one at a bustling café on Rose Street. An enormous Art- Deco chandelier hung sparkling and bright in the center of the room, and on every table sat a shiny cafetiere filled with aromatic black coffee. The place looked hip and popular, and I *knew* this was where I needed to be.

The manager was a dark-haired, dark-eyed, Scotsman of Irish descent who poured on the charm, smiling devilishly as he listened to my plight. I was hired as a waitress, earning just two Pounds an hour with no tips. The wage was offered "off the books" because I had no working visa. He promised to make me feel at home and show me his beautiful city.

His name was Robert and we spent all of our time together, fascinated with one another's past. Although we were young and not really in love we made a commitment, and several months later Robert agreed to marry me so that I could stay and work legally in the country. He dutifully accompanied me to the stuffy, institutional immigration offices where, after several visits of holding hands and exclaiming our love, I was issued a residency card. We couldn't manage a long-term relationship—though we tried—and after six months we separated and lost track of one another.

Meanwhile, the children had their own reactions to our big move —very different from mine and from one another.

Sleeping through the night was nearly impossible for Raine. He constantly had nightmares and developed tired, puffy bags under his sweet seven-year-old eyes. He also fought against his new school and its many rules.

He came home one afternoon during his first week, red-faced and angry. Violently, he tore off his blazer and threw it to the floor. He ripped the bright yellow-and blue-striped tie from his throat, wrestling it over his head, and slamming it in the heap with exaggerated vigor. He screamed, "They sent me to the stupid head master's office because I ate pizza with my fingers! I told those stupids,

THAT'S HOW YOU'RE SUPPOSED TO EAT IT! And I'm not using a stupid fork like a stupid sissy! And," he huffed, "they call me Ah-MAIRR-ick-an and say I have a tail and chase me around. Look," he said spinning around, "I told those stupids, I don't have a tail. I hate it here!"

He was no longer a toddler who didn't complain. He was a boy who'd been forced to give up his friends and his prized BMX bike and the toys he'd treasured because we couldn't bring everything. A boy who was already uncertain of life. I hadn't given him a stable home and the horrendous events in his young life shone bright in his wide green eyes, evidenced in a melancholy far too heavy for a child so young.

I'd focused so intently on survival that I failed to see the damage my son sustained, both from the trauma we'd escaped, and the neglect and abandonment at my own hands. I couldn't see the depth of his fear, distrust, and sadness - that would boil and fester for years. Anger billowed up from inside of him, exploding into a toxic cloud that would eventually threaten to destroy his life. Raine would struggle for years, developing a false bravado for protection. He fought me until his spirit was bruised and bloody. He fought until he found his own inner strength, truth, and a solid determination to love and be loved. But, as a seven-year-old boy in Scotland he began to exhibit behaviors that were the result of a confusing and tumultuous life.

Conversely, Elizabeth loved clutching her brother's hand while marching to the end of our gravel drive. Clad in a smart school uniform, they waited for the bus to deliver them to school. She was delighted with her pleated tartan skirt, gray tights, and crisp white blouse that all the girls wore. In her much younger class, she was not teased but admired for her golden hair and quick smile. Her teachers swooned over her, calling her, "A wee angel." She made friends easily and did not rail against the rules. As a youngster, she idolized her big brother and trusted him implicitly. That is until Raine began to take his anger out on her.

Elizabeth never forgot when a wrong was received, especially if her brother dished it out. As a toddler, she once cold-cocked him on the side of his head with a cowboy boot while he sat, unsuspecting, watching television. Apparently, days before he'd pinched her and taken away a toy that belonged to him, leaving her squalling on the floor. Her retribution wasn't swift but it was measured. Now, years later in Scotland, she plotted her revenge for his mistreatment by being the "good child." She followed rules and completed her studies while she watched her brother lie, and rebel against authority landing him, time and again, in hot water. Thus, the good girl-bad boy dichotomy was born.

Months after we arrived, my mother, having taken early retirement, came to Scotland to live with us. I was excited to have support and much-needed help with Elizabeth and Raine. We'd begun to build and strengthen our relationship during my ordeal with Aaron's arrest and trial.

"Nita!" my mother called from the top of the stairs, "Raine needs his school jacket and tie, and Elizabeth needs more knee socks picked up at Marks and Spencer today. I'll take them into Edinburgh and get them."

"Okay, thanks Mom. I'll have to work until nine tonight. I'll see you later."

We fostered a new respect for each other and I felt free to discover who I was without fear of disappointing her. She also supported and encouraged my abilities. She began to push me to learn more about them, a few months before our move from the U.S.

"You're not crazy," she said to me one night when I revealed stories of having *pictures* and hearing *voices*. We sat Indian style on the floor, face to face, and drank our second glass of wine. We talked late into the night. "You're psychic," my mother stated.

"But, how do you know?" I asked.

"Because, I've read about it and I have always *known* things myself."

"Really? Like what?"

"I don't know," she said and paused. "Like, I *knew* your father was cheating on me. I get feelings about people and I'm usually right. I *know* things about them that I shouldn't. I've always believed in past lives because I remember one of mine. I was an Indian and I had a horse that I felt so connected to. It was like he was my brother instead of an animal. I've known it since I was a child and Boots confirmed it for me in my reading. I have just always *known*."

"Why didn't you ever talk about that stuff?"

"I don't know." She paused. "I did a little with my friends. I didn't as much with you girls. I knew all of you had some ability, but I didn't realize how strong your gifts were. You need to give readings and open a center one day." I was floored by her response. I felt validated. I thought that maybe I wasn't crazy after all. I would one day give my first professional reading to a friend of my mother's.

I never imagined that my mother would not only support me but believe in me, too. It was a new experience for us both. After that night we talked about events in each of our pasts without judgment. We forgave and moved forward. We began the healing process, and built a relationship based on the present. For the first time I came to know my mother as a woman and adult.

When she arrived in Scotland we lived in the flat I'd rented which had an occupant that we were unaware of. Off the kitchen, under the stairway, was a pantry where we kept some canned goods, cleaning supplies, and the rubbish.

Occasionally, when the pantry door was opened a foul smell like a rotting animal would linger, seemingly out of nowhere. After a few weeks the rotten smell became more constant and I *knew* there was a presence in that pantry that was responsible for the offending odor. I could feel it. One morning when I pulled the door open a wall of energy rushed toward me. It felt like a strong pressure pushing me backward, followed by the stench. I stepped back in surprise and with my heart racing I screamed, "Okay enough! Get out! You are not welcome here."

The smell disappeared instantly and I *knew* I'd been right. But that wasn't the end of it. We began to hear loud banging late in the night that came from the crawl space above us and sometimes from the stairway.

The commotion would wake the children and Raine would call out in a frightened voice, "Mommy, what's that noise? It's scaring me. Is someone on the stairs?"

"It's okay, Raine, go back to sleep. It's just the house," I lied. The pesky invader continued to stink things up. I meditated, prayed, filled the house with light, and asked for angelic help to rid the space of the malicious spirit. Eventually, it left and not long after, we did too.

I secured a loan and bought a house that was a short train ride from Edinburgh. It was a "listed" building which meant it was historic. It'd been built in 1798 and was located at the bottom of the Pentland Hills. It had been completely refurbished on the interior and was situated on an acre of farmland that held the remnants of a stone carriage house at its borders. The views were breathtaking. I vowed I would never go back to the States, and I felt truly safe for the first time in years.

I landed a job at a four-red-star hotel as an assistant manageress. I'd been working in the hospitality industry since the age of seventeen, and I was well versed in service. Several months later I was hired to open and manage a pub and bistro from the ground up for a large brewery in Scotland. I hadn't carried such responsibility alone in the past, but I was determined to make things work. Failure was simply not in my vocabulary.

On my first day, I met my district manager at an abandoned stone building. The top floor was once a popular pub that boasted of serving Robert Frost his daily brew while he visited Scotland. I was given a chair, a phone, and a phonebook in an empty room with only the skeletal remains of an old and deeply scarred bar.

"There yi are luv," my district manager said with a smile. "Let me know how yi go. You'll need ti find a chef for the bistro below, as well as staff. We will take care of the opening inventory for the pub. No worries there." And with that, he was gone. I had to figure everything out for myself. Fortunately, I did.

The most valuable item I brought to Scotland was a dog-eared book my mother had given me years before named, *You Can Heal Your Life* by Louise L. Hay. As a teenager, when I attempted the positive affirmations suggested in the book, my stomach would lurch and I'd think, *you're such a liar and so full of shit.* I'd stop and look away, disgusted with my reflection.

Now, years later, I realized I had debilitating and negative thought patterns that ran in my mind day and night. I began to hear my thoughts, *I am weird and don't fit in. People don't like me. I am ugly. I am a bad mother. I am cheap and stupid. If people knew the things I have done, I would disgust them.* On and on the thinking process went. So, each time I had a hateful thought about myself, I replaced it with a loving one like, *I am beautiful. People are drawn to me. I am a good mother, and I love and approve of myself. I am not crazy. I am worthy of love.* I taped my affirmations all over my house and I carried one in my wallet. Every time I passed a mirror, I spoke a loving statement about myself and blocked out any negative response. Sometimes, tears filled my eyes as I spoke my affirmations. My throat closed and I fought the urge to look away. I wanted my children to learn to love themselves and I knew it had to start with me.

Over time, with perseverance, I began to like myself. I embraced a transformation of who I *knew* I could be. It was born first with Raine and then with Elizabeth. I discovered that being a battered child, drug addict, neglectful mother, or victim of rape did not have to define me. Rather, all my experiences were purposeful, and I could find strength and meaning in them. I could decide who I'd become. *You can create your life, you can. Who do you want to be?*

Scotland was my home now, and the girl I'd been before disappeared. She belonged to another life I no longer lived. I would, however, revisit it again and again in an attempt to heal and forgive myself. The process would take decades of conscious exercises to release self-doubt, blame, rejection, and hate.

But to begin, I listened more attentively to the voice within and I learned to trust in the flow of life. I recognized that the *voice* I'd heard for so many years came from me--my divinity, my intuition. It was my connection with God. It was my very soul.

Once I started to meditate and converse with the *light-body,* that I now called my father guide, I no longer saw it hovering outside of me.

It was the decision to change that began my transformation. A simple decision to heal and forgive. The key was in learning to trust. If I could trust in myself and my process, the understanding would follow.

One afternoon, nearly a year after my mother had moved to Scotland, we stood huddled against the icy wind on a train platform, waiting for the Waverly to deliver us into Edinburgh. My mom had decided to return to the U.S. and had already purchased her flight. She wanted to stock up on items she couldn't buy in the States before she left. Her neck was wrapped with a thick scarf that covered her mouth as she spoke. "I'm going to stay with Maggie, Ronnie and the kids until I can find a place of my own. I certainly won't miss this weather," she said with a smile that lit her eyes.

I'd recently accepted a new job as the manager of a trendy restaurant in the city of Glasgow, which I was to start two weeks later. I was sad to see my mother go, but had no intention of returning with her. Yet, as my mother talked of her plans, I heard the *voice*. *If you stay and don't return with your mother, you may regret your choice.* The *voice* went on. *It's time to go now, time to go home.*

Hell no, I thought. *I'm never going back!* But I *knew* the voice was right. Although I didn't want to go, and was terrified with the idea of it, for some reason I *knew* I had to. I reluctantly sold all that I owned and bought three one-way tickets to California. Maggie would have a full house.

12

S leeping homeless people crowded every open doorway and
  overhang. They lay on tattered cardboard mats and newspaper. The lucky were wrapped in blankets or sleeping bags
while others huddled under layered clothing, their heads covered in
wooly caps. Sidewalks and gutters saturated with smell of urine could
not be escaped in the damp morning air.

The San Francisco sky was heavy with fog that left a cloud of
moisture clinging to my face as I walked to Pete's for my morning
espresso. As I approached the street corner, a homeless man sat up
and leaned against the doorway of where he'd slept. Jumbled in a
heap beside him-- in a filthy burrow of despair-- was fishing net
stuffed with clothes, a torn plastic Safeway bag that brimmed with
crushed aluminum cans, and his bedding in a tangled mass of
guarded treasure. His feet were bare and blackened with street grime,
his toenails shockingly yellow and long. The odor of his unwashed
body wafted toward me, in the mist. Webbed with deep cracks that
looked raw and painful, his swollen hands shook as he carefully
opened a pint-sized bottle and lifted it reverently to his lips.

I watched the man and thought, *What a shame. Poor man, what a
waste.* - The *voice* was immediate. *Who are we, to judge our brother?*

Perhaps a hundred people pass by him today, forever changed by his presence. Can it be his gift to us? Does he live exactly as his soul intends? How can we know? I was stung with the arrogance of my thoughts and felt embarrassment spread to my cheeks. I believed my thoughts were compassionate and didn't see the judgment in them. The homeless man stared blankly into the street, caught in his own reverie as I passed. After that morning, when I found myself judging others, thinking that I knew a better path for them, I remembered the *voice* and worked hard to look within to discover what my real fear was. That was just one way my gifts helped me grow and develop.

Having the Clairs impacted my life in other unique ways. I'd developed a different filter in which I saw the world. I didn't feel like my life happened to me, leaving me helpless or without choice. Rather, I understood that every event had meaning and held a specific lesson for me. My life was a series of soul agreements that were mutually beneficial, even the traumatic ones. Even rape.

To be clear, I didn't pop up one morning and exclaim, "Today's a good day for a rape!" It was in no way my fault. I didn't ask for it. But every thought I had, all the beliefs about myself, led me to that possible moment. What I did with the experience was up to me.

When I looked back at my life, I realized that the information had always been there, but that my own self- doubt and youth had prohibited me from fully understanding. Honestly, i t took years to heal and peel back the layers of fear, anger, and misunderstanding. And it took work.

In Scotland, I accepted my gifts and myself, helping me to understand that I had a choice. I could choose to use my abilities or I could continue to ignore them. I chose to use not only my natural abilities, but to learn how to master my skill. That required patience, trust, and practice, practice, practice. I had to walk my talk.

I went over why I had decided to go back to Aaron, and the reasons were many. The heart of it lay in the rejection of myself and what I *knew* or felt. I held a deep-seated belief that I wasn't good enough, coupled with a comfort level with abuse. Violence and emotional battering seemed normal to me. I falsely thought the behavior was love. Even greater than this, was a soul agreement with my children. They too had agreements to be biologically connected with Aaron, and the reasons for that are not important for me to know. They, like all of us, have individual soul intent and these aspects are reflections of their life paths and what they choose to learn and experience. We are all linked together. We are all one.

The more I prayed and meditated and gave readings, the stronger my gifts became. The trick was learning to trust my ability. I gave psychic readings much in the same way I had with Angie, hearing words in my mind coupled with that deeper *knowing*. Of course with time, my technique was refined.

I'd start with silent prayer and intent, asking for a clear and open channel of information. I'd ask for support and guidance from my client's angels and guides. I'd ask to align my highest source with theirs. Through vibration of name, I connected with the energy, that was my client, and the information flowed in through words, feelings, smells, and visions.

I would learn to channel loved ones who'd passed on and transitioned to another consciousness. In the beginning, some who died would find me, invading my home, moving objects, making noise to gain my attention. Or they simply manifested in front of me, talking so fast I'd run for paper and pen. They hoped I might deliver a message to their families or loved ones. Some of the souls I had known in life and others I hadn't. I am grateful for my gifts and couldn't imagine a life without them, but, as you know, it wasn't always easy.

I'd been reluctant to return to the U.S., but the guidance I received on the train platform that day was a blessing.

When we arrived back in the States, we lived temporarily with Maggie and her family, who opened their home and welcomed us in. Maggie was married with three children and genuinely happy. Their little three-bedroom ranch was crowded because there were five extra people instead of just four. My friend and employee, Helen, had also come with us. I told her of my plans to return home and her response surprised me.

"You'll never believe what I've decided," I confided as we walked to the train station after work.

"What?" she asked.

"I've decided to go back to the States with my mum. I can't let her go alone. I just have a feeling about it."

"Ken I cum wit ye then?" She asked with eyes full of hope. "I'll pey ye back fer my ticket. I will. I've not been to America and I really need a new start."

"Yeah. Sure. Why not? We'll ask my sister if you can stay with us."

"Eewww!" she squealed. "Oh thank ye, thank ye!" she said, as she squeezed my neck dancing from toe to toe.

The truth was that I was terrified to leave Scotland, and Helen offered a chance to bring it with me. I had a new last name, new friends, and a brogue. These things helped me to feel safe.

I can never let him find us. No one can connect me with the girl of my past. That was how things needed to be for my children's protection. I would keep the whole truth about our past secret from most people for decades.

I slept on the top bunk in Maggie's boy's room and Helen took the bottom. I lay in bed night after night meditating and visualizing a new job that would support us. I *knew* I would find something perfect, and only weeks later, I landed a job as the director of operations with a growing restaurant chain. I opened six restaurants with them, and wrote training material for all levels.

The first job in my new position was to open an upscale opera café that was weeks away from completion. There, I met a man named Dylan.

I hurried through the dining room, still under construction, trying to avoid scattered tools, wooden sawhorses and workmen. The shrill screech of the skill-saw used to cut marble tile assaulted my eardrums and bounced from every hard and incomplete surface. The walls had yet to be covered with rich, dark, mahogany woods to match the ornate bar. The floors were to be laid in veined marble squares, polished to a sparkling sheen that supported luxurious booths and tables covered with crisp white linens. The room would be finished with a beautiful Steinway grand piano.

I moved toward the bar, my arms aching with bulky manuals and heavy paperwork. I realized too late that a fine dust from cut marble and wood blanketed the bar's top. It clung to my suit's sleeves, puffing up in a great cloud as I tried in vain to wipe it away. Swatting wildly, I attempted to clear the air as I scanned the room for Tim, the bar manager. Irritated, I spun around and nearly fell into our executive chef, Dylan. He stood behind me clutching a clipboard to his chest. In a mock Elvis voice he said, "Well, excuse me, little lady." His head teetered back and forth as he smiled.

Dylan was tall, well-muscled, and oh-so handsome. His laughing eyes were blue-gray and the man was funny—gut splitting, face hurting, wet-your-pants funny. That first time I saw him I felt something warm and familiar. He carried an air of self- confidence, a man comfortable in his own skin. I found him wildly attractive. He was sarcastic and he tickled me with his quick wit and clever remarks.

"Have you seen Tim?" I asked, gazing upward, forcing myself to keep a straight face and ignore his remark.

"He's probably drooling and hiding in a closet somewhere. He's terrified of you." Dylan answered, smiling.

"Is he now?" *Smart-ass.*

"Yeah, since you ripped him a new one he ran screaming from the building. He's probably in Texas by now."

"Ha, ha. Quite funny aren't yi?" I conceded grinning like a drooling fool.

"Well, we try, ma'am."

Because of our positions and workload, Dylan and I spent an inordinate amount of time together during the opening. We found ourselves crowded in the tiny manager's office filling out endless piles of paperwork and talking on separate phone extensions. We camped at dust-covered tables where I wrote training material and Dylan interviewed and hired staff. We organized pantry shelves and completed opening inventories. We were the first ones to arrive each morning and the last ones to leave at night.

One night after work, I offered to drive us into town for a pizza dinner. My car was an old beat-up Buick Skylark. I parked directly in front of the pizza joint located in an affluent downtown area where my vehicle looked like a rotten tooth in an otherwise perfect smile. As we approached the car after eating, Dylan began waving his arms like an orangutan and dancing from foot to foot. "Be careful now folks!" he shouted to strangers on the sidewalk. "Be careful! Step back now. You never know if she'll blow on ignition."

He wore a goofy smirk on his face and his laughing eyes sparkled with delight as he teased me publicly about my old beater. I laughed and laughed at his brazen behavior. Another time, Dylan gave me a lift to the store. We'd finished work and were meeting several co-workers for drinks. "I'll be right back," I said. I ran into the market to buy Ex-Lax for obvious reasons and as I stood in line to check out, Dylan was suddenly at my side. He glanced down at the conveyer belt and my cheeks began to sizzle with embarrassment. He scooped up the Ex-Lax and shouted, "Oh-boy! Ex-lax! Who needs it?!" He waved his arm over his head capturing the attention of the shoppers and anyone in earshot. "Ex-Lax here! Anyone need it?" The checker and I laughed hysterically along with everyone in line. What was I going to do with him?

"I know she's out there so-omewhere, on the western sky- yline." Bruce Hornsby blasted in Dylan's RX-7 as we cruised down the highway to a secret destination only Dylan knew. The night before, we'd sat together in a trendy California bar, crowded with patrons hoping to satisfy their hunger by connecting with that special some-one. Dylan leaned forward and spoke softly in my ear, "I want to be with you. I don't want you to see anyone else." He pulled away and regarded me with his blue-gray eyes.

My stomach fluttered with delight. "Okay," I smiled. "But you might be in for it." I teased.

We began our exploration of one another.

Dylan was the sixth of ten children, raised back east in a conserv-ative household. Recognizing intuition or understanding the Clairs was new for him. He did confess that while he respected the Catholic faith he'd grown up in, it didn't feel like his truth. Dylan was always very intuitive.

As we spent time together, he took care to hold my past and pain gently, protecting me while applying his love, humor, and understanding like a lifesaving salve. He was the first person I trusted to tell all my secrets to and he did not judge or condemn me. Instead, he embraced all that I was. It didn't matter to him that I had two children out of wedlock, or that I could not have anymore because of a hysterectomy years before. Nor did it matter that my mother and I lived together and that wouldn't change. My past and all that it entailed mattered not at all to Dylan.

One night as we lay together talking he said, "I knew I would meet a blonde woman that would change my life when I opened this restaurant. And then, there you were and I knew it was you."

"Really?" I responded with surprise. Boy, I was starting to fall for this guy.

Helen couldn't work without a visa so she helped with the children and explored her new world. She moved out six months later, seeking her own friends and a new life. We lost contact and I never knew what became of her.

I'd also lost contact with my father when I went back to Aaron. I knew he remarried again twice after divorcing Della'Rae. He still lived in the South near his brother and other extended family.

Several months after I'd left Louisiana, my stepbrother, Harry, died in a motorcycle accident. The accident occurred on June 10th, my father's birthday and my half-sister, Sarah's, first birthday. The day it happened I was back in California in a car with Aaron. I felt energy like an electric current move through me. "Oh my, God," I said. "I feel death. Someone has died."

I wouldn't know that it was Harry until I phoned my father at the end of that week. "Dad, is everyone okay?" I asked.

"No." he said. "Harry died. He wrecked his motorcycle last week. He was brain dead and we had to let him go."

"Why didn't you call me? You knew we were friends. I can't believe you wouldn't call me!"

"I'm sorry. I just didn't think about it." I felt grief and regret in the vibration of his voice.

A year before Harry's death, my father and Della'Ray had a little girl together. Her conception was nothing short of a miracle for Della'Ray who'd had her tubes tied ten years before.

My half-sister, Sarah, was raised as an only child. I did my best to build a relationship with her and stay in contact. Sarah is twenty years my junior and only a year older than Elizabeth.

She lived a difficult life, filled with poverty and struggle. She worked hard to overcome adversity and became a professional model. She is happily married and resides near me in Arizona. Sarah also possesses some Clairs, most strongly, Claircognizance.

My other three sisters live in close proximity to one another, and get together for holidays and special events. Karina had three children and raised her family in the Mormon faith. She is a gifted quilt maker and lives a happy and grounded life. She is an exceptional mother and I admire her immensely. Karina is blessed with several Clairs and can still make people squirm just by fixing them with her *knowing* green eyes that say, *I can see you.*

Isla has two children and raised them as a single mother. She struggled for years with a crippling learning disability that left her feeling socially awkward and scarcely able to read or write. Yet, against all odds, she managed to make friends, hold steady jobs, and support her family. She works with horses, practicing the Parelli method and using her special gift as a way of communicating. I fondly call her "Doctor Doolittle."

Maggie raised her three children and remains happily married. She has two Standard Schnauzers that she breeds and shows professionally. Oh, how she loves those dogs. We talk often and have stayed close.

Aaron remains incarcerated and has at least seventy years left on his sentence. I saw him only once after his arrest. I'd gone to the jail where he was held to ask him why he had done the things he was accused of.

Aaron shuffled, unsteady in handcuffs and ankle chains, to a chair in a small cage enclosed in Plexiglas. He wore a bright orange jumpsuit with numbers in bold black stenciling across his back. My heart pumped wildly and my hands were frozen. I felt ethereal, like an apparition of myself, as I picked up the receiver in the booth where I sat.

Aaron immediately started to ramble, "I didn't do it. I'm being set up by those motherfuckers. Just read the police reports. The guy they're looking for was described as a Mexican or a black man. A fucking Mexican. It wasn't me, they're setting me up."

Aaron's mouth was dry and his eyes were glassy and dilated. He had a faraway look as though he was somewhere else. I realized he was. I couldn't respond. I felt trapped in time, literally unable to move. The Aaron I'd known was no longer present, he was completely gone. I didn't know the stranger who sat before me and I wanted to run, to bolt from the room, to exorcise the very existence of this man. As I looked into his eyes, the Aaron I had known, slipped away. What I saw within him deeply disturbed and frightened me. I'd secretly harbored hope that maybe he really didn't do it. I did not want Aaron to be a rapist, but any hope I had flew away. I know what I saw and it left no room for doubt.

I was unable to ask him why. I spoke only once saying, "I have to go now." I stood on shaky legs, exiting the room and never looking back. We have had no contact since that day, nor have the children expressed any interest in having any connection with him or his family.

I also never made contact with Aaron's ex-girlfriend, who I'd only met only once all those years ago at his house. Raine and Elizabeth have a half-brother somewhere and I imagine him happy and well.

Dylan and I dated monogamously for a year during which we fell in love. We decided to move in together and see where things went. My mother also lived with us and worked part- time. Dylan and my mother loved one another and got on well. It seemed we'd begun to build a family together.

After a year we relocated to the east coast. We had lived there for a year when my mother returned to California with a cancerous brain tumor. She died at age fifty-six, only four years after our return from Scotland and one month after my wedding to Dylan.

I still see and hear her frequently. It was my mother who pushed me to write this book some ten years before I committed to writing full time. We were living in Kennebunkport, Maine, and I was alone in my room when I felt her presence. She said, "It's time you wrote your book."

"I can't. I don't know how to start or what to say." "Just put a pen to paper and it will come."

I sat still and sighed.

"There's a pad next to the bed in your room. Go get it, Nita, and get started."

That was how I began.

Dylan and I sat eating dinner that night and I said, "My mom was here today and she had a great idea for us."

Dylan's face lit up and he replied, "Really? How is Caroline? Is she good? What did she say?" That's how Dylan responded to me, unquestioning my odd gifts.

We lived in Virginia for nine years, during which time we were married. Dylan wanted to adopt the Raine and Elizabeth but we discovered, that in our case, adoption was not in the best interest of the children. Because I'd never married Aaron, paternity had to be proven, which meant Aaron would be contacted in jail, and our whereabouts would be revealed. This would once again place us in danger. We went to court where a judge, in an order of protection, sealed the children's birth certificates, supplied them with new Social Security numbers, and legally changed their surnames to Dylan's in an attempt to keep them safe from their biological father. I'd presented a letter from the prosecutor' s office that explained what had happened when I'd fled the country. It read in part:

Ms. McKenna was an essential source of information in the investigation of Aaron Goddard. She was also an important witness against him at trial. Mr. Goddard was well aware of the role of Ms. McKenna and indicated that her life would be in danger if he was ever released. After Mr. Goddard was convicted and incarcerated in state prison, his former cell mate of his made attempts to contact Ms. McKenna. These included the apparent theft of court documents and records. This happened on at least one occasion and may very well have involved several other occasions. Additionally we received information that the defendant threatened to have other persons in and out of state prison also attempt to locate Ms. McKenna. It is my belief that Aaron Goddard could be a grave threat to Ms. McKenna if she is located...

The letter referred to the men who came to my house with guns in an obvious attempt to do harm. Both, Raine and Elizabeth know the truth of their paternity, but for them Dylan was and is their father. Throughout their lives he administered his special brand of love, patience, and laughter, and helped them to become strong, steady people.

Elizabeth can always be counted on to get her father's jokes and mirrors his lightning wit and sense of humor, while Raine inherited Dylan's thought process.

Raine went through a period of angry defiance, sneaking out of windows, cutting school, and fighting authority. Yet he overcame his adversity and grew into a man who is self-aware and always trying to improve himself. Raine possesses a strong ability for Clairvoyance.

He married quite young and fathered a daughter, who is a stunning and sweet child. She dubbed me "Sugar," and what better gift could I ask for than to be called such a sweet name? She, too, shares some Clairs, the *knowing* or Claircognizance most strongly. I remain eager to watch other Clairs unfold.

Elizabeth always followed the rules but had her own struggles. She, like many of us, fights with low self-esteem. Elizabeth had to find worth within herself and is now a strong woman who knows her own mind. She was born with all of the Clairs but prefers to do nothing to strengthen or enhance her ability. She married in her mid-twenties and gave birth to a daughter. This child is gifted with all of the Clairs as well, and is beautiful and strong like her mother.

When Delilah, Elizabeth's daughter, was born, I had been there to help. One morning while mother and baby slept, I slipped out to take a run. I jogged beneath the shade of tall trees, surrounded in the cool morning air when I became aware of my mother's presence. Smiling, I addressed her in my mind. *Hi, Mom. Isn't Delilah beautiful?*

Yes, and when you look into her eyes you'll see an aspect of me. We share soul intent. I have come with her.

What? I asked stopping my run. *How can that be?*

Remember Nita, we are all one. I don't have to re-incarnate to have life experience. We share our experience in the same way we share with our guides, our higher self. Some would say that I'm one of her guides. The lessons I learn on other levels of consciousness are available to Delilah should she choose to access them.

Of course. Why haven't I ever thought of it like that?

It was my illusion that we are all separate and the belief that there is something greater than ourselves, that we don't have access to, or we are not worthy of, kept my limited thinking alive.

The information felt right to me, although I knew i t was in absolute opposition to what most people believed. But, then again, most of my experiences are hard for others to believe.

Raine and Elizabeth are close today and share an apartment. They moved in together two years after Elizabeth and her husband separated. They each struggle with the past and try to support one another as best they can. They are learning who they are as adults and working hard to find their way.

Dylan and I remain together and truly happy. Our lives are filled with laughter, thanks to Dylan's wit and good humor. We feel blessed for our time together. He is my constant inspiration. His love dared me to stand in my truth and step unflinching into my power. When I worried what his family and others might think he would say, "Don't worry about what people think. Be who you are. You have a gift. Don't hide it, use it. I don' t care what people think." He is an exceptional man and I am a lucky, lucky girl.

While living in Arizona I was invited to speak to a woman's group about intuition. I wanted to explain the Clairs for them, so that they might recognize their own ability. I struggled to isolate instances that were so common-place for me. Elizabeth, who was an adult and a mother herself, helped me to organize my thoughts in a conversation one afternoon.

"I need help," I said into the phone, "I'm trying to think of examples of each Clair for a talk I'm giving and I' m struggling with it."

"What part?" she asked.

"All of it. It's hard to break it down. I think I'm making it more complicated than it is. Maybe I should skip it," I said.

"No, don't do that. I think it's important to explain it," she said. "Tell me again, each Clair, because I grew up with this stuff and I still get confused. Like what's the one called when you hear voices or when you can hear Gran talk to you even though she's dead?"

"Clairaudience," I answered quickly.

"Okay, audio, I get that one," she replied. "What's the one that gives you pictures? You know, the one you passed on to your innocent children, where we can see people who are dead or those flashes in our mind of what's coming? Or worse, when you traumatized us by seeing things in your magical little mind that a normal parent wouldn't have been able to see."

"Cute, Elizabeth, you two are definitely not innocent. Anyway, that's Clairvoyance."

"Yes, I think that one is more familiar to people because they have heard it before. Which Clair is it that you said is so common, the one where you can smell? Like when I swear I can smell Gran or that time in Scotland when the pantry smelled like rotting trash? Remember that? Totally creepy."

"Yes, I remember," I replied, picturing the pantry in my mind. "That is called Clairellience. That's a hard one to remember."

"Okay, so there's what, three out of five?" "Yep."

"I think the easiest one is the *knowing* or what us normal people call 'gut' instinct. Everyone has experienced intuition at least once. When you just have a feeling about something random and it turns out you were right. Don't tell me, I know this one. Clair—um, Clair--"

"Cognizant," I interrupted. "Claircognizant."

"Yes! It was on the tip of my tongue. Thanks for that, I almost had it. Now, how about the one I'm good at? The one where I know what a person is really feeling."

"That, my dear, is Clairsentient," I replied, tickled at the smile of pride in her voice.

"See. That was easy right? Just say that."

Amused with my daughter, I said, "Thanks, Elizabeth. What would I do without you?"

"You'd be lost," she replied.

It has taken most of my adult life to tell my story and not be afraid for my children. I asked their permission to reveal our past and both said similar things. Raine replied, "Just tell the story, Mom. I'm not afraid and I'm proud of our past. I'm proud of you."

Elizabeth said, "I think you have to tell the whole thing because it will help other people. Others need to know that they can overcome anything. Tell it. I'm not afraid."

I am so proud of our children and the people they have become, and I owe them a debt of gratitude for bringing me to my truth. They are my greatest teachers and the largest catalyst of change in my life.

I have stayed true to my story and the way in which the events unfolded. I hope that by telling it, I have in no way hurt or brought pain to those women who showed incredible courage and perseverance in testifying all those years ago.

I believe we each have a unique path and truth that are inextricably linked. Because our truths might be different does not make any one of us wrong. On the contrary, our truths are exactly right for each of us. Our choices aren't right or wrong, they simply reflect what we are seeking to learn and our soul intent. We are always where we need to be, learning what we need to learn.

Healing starts with the decision to heal. It is the letting go of judgment and the allowing of forgiveness. If we can start with that, we are on our way.

EPILOGUE

Invisible fear filled my lungs as I ran in terror on cramped legs. All that I could remember was that I had to hide. Aaron was chasing me—he'd been released from prison in a cruel and blundering oversight. *Please don't let him take my children God. Please,* I thought in a panic. *Did I hide them well enough?*

I strained to see in the darkness when suddenly I realized that Elizabeth was on the path ahead of me. Her blonde hair lit up like a halo in the moon's soft light. I tried to scream, "No! Elizabeth. Hide!" but my mouth gapped open like a fissure and made no sound at all.

In the next suffocating moment I heard Elizabeth's voice, "Mommy?" she cried, holding her arms aloft. "Mommy, I'm scared." And then Aaron was upon her. His ski mask pulled snugly over his face, revealing only eyes. As he leaned down to pick her up my screams shook me out of a deep and disturbing sleep.

My heart swelled and drummed against my ribs. Adrenalin left me aching. Dylan's shadow spilled across the floor. "Are you okay?" he asked, stepping into our room. Still shaken, I replied, "I'm okay." We had only been married a few months but Dylan was already familiar with my nightmares. The bed eased under his weight and I rolled toward him. "I heard you scream," he said. "Were you having another bad dream?"

"It was Aaron." I replied near tears. "He was chasing me and he tried to take Elizabeth. I couldn't find a place to hide."

Dylan placed his warm hand against my shoulder reassuring me with his touch. "It was just a dream, babe. You're okay."

Fear and anger dominated my sleep. I felt foolish and weak. I had no control over my dreams- dreams that I knew couldn't hurt me in reality, yet hurled me into terror night after night. I'd had recurring nightmares for years now. And not just about Aaron. I had dreams that I would explode into fits of rage, shaking and beating – an inconceivable thought in my waking life. These nightmares left me with a deep sense of guilt and shame. *Why am I still so afraid?* I thought. *Will I always be broken? Will it drive Dylan away?* I worried.

I thought that I'd moved on, but I *knew* deep down that I continued to hold on to the past. I had survived by looking forward, getting through another day. My need to be with Aaron hadn't been random. An absent and dysfunctional father, along with the anger and blame I held for him, were at the root of my problem. I'd known it for years. Thoughts of my father were like acid that eroded my being. I never thought of Aaron. I had that part of my life behind me. *Wasn't that enough?*

If I can forgive my father, I thought, maybe I can forgive Aaron. Maybe I can forgive myself. But how do I release my fear? How do I forgive? I wondered. I hadn't realized the utter exhaustion of what I carried.

I took my question into meditation. *How do I forgive and release my fear?* No immediate answer appeared, but I stayed open, waiting for guidance. It came in the most mundane way.

At a health food store a few days later, I heard voices from the next aisle over, "I'm using intention to bring in abundance," a woman said. "I'm so sick of being broke."

"How are you doing it?" her friend asked.

"You know, affirming that I deserve abundance every day." And suddenly, I had my answer. *Use conscious intention.*

Applying conscious intent meant mindfully choosing an intention each day, such as, *My intention is to forgive my father.* It is the act of bringing the thought into the conscious moment. By doing this we create intent, and that intent has power. *Our intention is everything.* I made a decision and began a daily practice.

I could not predict how I would come to see my father and our relationship as I applied conscious intent. I thought that by deciding to forgive, the anger, blame, and fear would simply melt away. But that isn't what happened at all.

One morning as we stood outside, Dylan pointed and said, "Look at that fungus on the roof." I followed the direction of his finger tilting back my head and shading my eyes. "I've never even seen that," I said surprised.

"We need to call someone. Can you find some companies and get quotes? We need to take care of this," Dylan said as he got into his car to go to work. *He looks so handsome in his chef whites*, I thought. "Dylan Lapinski, Executive Chef" was embroidered above his left breast pocket.

"I'll take care of it." I said.

Two weeks later on a Monday morning, two trucks pulled up in front of our house. I'd interviewed four companies and decided on a small, local business for the job. Three men dressed in white painter pants and t-shirts neatly arranged their tools in groups on the driveway. Five-gallon buckets, piles of rags torn and frayed, containers of chemicals, and hard bristled brushes were lined up. The owner, Owen Hayes lifted a small motor with a long, metal wand attached by tubing from the truck. The passenger door swung open revealing a young boy with an Admirals hat on. The Admirals were a local AHL hockey team wildly popular with kids.

The boy had blond hair and blue eyes like his dad, and looked to be around seven-years- old. Clutched in his right fist was a Superman figurine. He spotted the meager shade of our newly planted tree in the front yard and sat beneath it. "Sheeeew, sheeew," came the sound from his lips as he lifted his super hero into the air, flying into imaginary worlds.

Several hours had passed when I peeked out of the window and saw that the boy was alone under the tree. *I wonder if he's hungry or needs the bathroom*, I thought. *It's really getting hot.* I stepped from the cool house into the rising heat of the day. Squatting beside the boy I asked, "What's your name?"

"Jack," he answered squinting up at me. His lips parted, showing two missing front teeth.

"Are you hungry Jack? Would you like a snack or to use the bathroom?"

"What kinda snack?"

"Oh, I don't know. I think I have some fruit or crackers. We can go inside and look, alright?"

He shrugged and said, "Sure, I guess so." I looked up on the roof and no one was paying any attention to us. I took Jacks hand and led him inside. "I'm Miss Nita, Jack. Let's see what we have."

Two hours passed before there was a knock on my door. "I sure hope you have Jack in here," Owen said with an easy smile.

"Yes, he's watching TV. I brought him inside to give him a snack and let him use the bathroom. He is probably ready for lunch."

"Oh, right. Okay. I guess I'll have to go pick something up." Are you kidding, I thought. *You come here with your kid and dump him on the lawn with no snack and no lunch in the heat?*

"It's okay," I said. "I can make him something."

"That'd be great. Thanks," Owen said, stepping off the porch. He said nothing to his child, who sat crossed legged in front of the television. Jack never even looked up.

The same pattern continued over the next two days and by the end of the third, I was seething. Who does he think he is? Just dumps that poor child off every day and expects me to feed and entertain him. What a complete ass. And we are paying him! He should pay me. What a joke! My thoughts were angry and judgmental. I felt no compassion and never considered the father's struggle. I didn't care. Hatred rolled in my stomach. I chewed him out over and over in my mind. I can't believe you're allowed to have this child! You should be ashamed of yourself just abandoning your son. It looks like you couldn't care less. What kind of parent does that?

It was in that moment that I saw it. Suddenly I realized that it wasn't Owen that I was angry with. I had gotten exactly what I'd asked for. The universe delivered a replica of my father at my door. Shock stung me as I realized, *he looks like my father and that little boy is me.* Not only did the man resemble my father, but he behaved like him too. And I'd picked him out of all the rest.

I saw my father and my life with him through a different lens. I saw that he was just a man. He had no idea how to be a parent. He had no malice. I understood that like Owen, my father loved me and wanted me to be taken care of, he just couldn't do it himself. It had nothing to do with me. It was all about *him* and his own limits. I was grateful yet taken back by my insight—it immediately changed how I felt.

I realized that my feelings of anger, hurt, and rejection had no effect on my father. He probably felt that he's tried to do his best.

It was my struggle alone. I discovered that *I am worth loving. Nothing is wrong with me.* It was a huge revelation and after that, I found I could begin to forgive. That day was the first step on a long walk of understanding and letting go.

The beauty and strength of working on ourselves is that we can't be sure in what way our answers will come. But if we ask, they assuredly will come.

CONSCIOUS INTENT

We all experience fearful, negative, thoughts, limiting beliefs, habitual behavior and feelings of unworthiness. One way to shift these debilitating patterns is to use *conscious intention.*

Practicing conscious thought, or intent, leads to a greater understanding of our experiences and ourselves, thus allowing us to heal. To use it is simple. First, choose your intent such as, releasing fear, judgment, anger, sadness, or criticism. Or you may choose to respond with love, acceptance, understand ing, compassion or grace.

The exercise can be done in five minutes or you can incorporate it with meditation for longer periods. Find a comfortable place to sit or recline. Focus on breath as it fills your lungs to capacity, and then simply let it go. Notice your body relax with each exhale. Stay with your breath for several minutes. Bring your focus from your mind's eye to the center of your chest. Feel this area expand and open like a flower. You may feel fluttering, tingling, or tightening. You may even feel mild pain. Stay with your breath while you focus on the heart center. Feel love flow from your heart out into the world. Breathe that energy for a few moments.

Next, mentally speak your intent, "I release: fear, anger, resentment, sadness etc." or "I respond with: love, compassion, patience, understanding, etc." Repeat your intent as you breathe. Visualize a funnel of light that begins at your heart center and opens upward toward the heavens. Affirm your connection with God, spirit, or divine self. Breathe. When you're ready, close your hands and hold the energy within you. Know that you will carry your intention throughout the day. If during your day you forget to practice your intention, don't worry, simply reaffirm your intention mentally and anchor the thought in your heart.

ABOUT THE AUTHOR

Nita Lapinski has been a working clairvoyant-medium for over three decades and offer's meditation classes and workshops on forgiveness, releasing judgment and finding one's intuition. She is a certified hypnotherapist and has studied integrative breath work and bio-energy. Both are modalities of healing emotional issues using breath and moving energy.

Nita resides in Arizona with her husband. *The Knowing* is her first book.

www.nitalapinski.com.
nitalapinski@gmail.com